A GOLDFISH IN THE MURKY POOL

Martin Hickes

Martin Hickes

A Goldfish in The Murky Pool

More Selected Journalism from
Yorkshire and beyond
2006~2011

MARTIN HICKES

DEDICATION

For all the Porters, Hickeses and Powells

"Space is big. You just won't believe how vastly, hugely, mind-bogglingly big it is. I mean, you may think it's a long way down the road to the chemist's, but that's just peanuts to space.

Douglas Adams, The Hitchhiker's Guide to the Galaxy

Martin Hickes

CONTENTS

1. HERE THERE BE DRAGONS
What lurks beneath the depths of Lake Windermere?

2. THE PRINCESS OF FINSTHWAITE
Do the remains of a lost Stuart lie lie in sleepy Lakeland?

3. ANTARCTICA IN FOCUS

4. REALITY AIN'T WHAT IT USED TO BE
Is the universe made up of 'quantum information.'

5. MASTERS OF THE UNIVERSE
A delve into a major restrospective on quantum physics.

6 SETTING SAIL FOR THE STARS
A new space sail takes shape.

7. BARACK OBAMA AND THE ART OF RHETORIC

8. THE GHOST OF DICKENS YORKSHIRE PAST

9. STAR OF WONDER?
Have scientists finally discovered the Star of Bethlehem?

10. SHEDDING NEW LIGHT ON ILKLEY MOOR

11. TURKEY, TRIMMINGS AND 22CTS.
Marco Pierre White muses on the gold plated turkey.

12. RIGHT ON TRACK FOR ART SUCCESS

13. THE LOST BOW
An ancient longbow is unearthed in Wharfedale.

14. A TOUCH OF G AND S IN THE NIGHT

15. RICHARD III UNDER FIRE

16. THOU ART FIRED
Do Shakespeare's plays contain a blueprint for business?

17. NOTHING NEW WHEN IT COMES TO POLITICAL CHANGE
Written at the time of the General Election.

18. THE NEW KID ON THE COMPUTER BLOCK

19. TAKEN AT THE FLOOD

20. TRIPLE CHEERS IN LONG PRESTON

21. A PASSPORT TO PERIL OR PROSPERITY

22. WHATEVER HAPPENED TO THE SOUTH SEA BUBBLE?

23. A WALK IN THE WOODS

24. A GOLDFISH IN THE MURKY POOL

25. WAS LIFE SEEDED FROM SPACE?

26. BLUES FOR THE RED PLANET

27. HAS LIGHT SPEED FINALLY BEEN SURPASSED?

28. A NEW TWIST ON ROYAL LINEAGE

29. THE RIVALS

30 THE EMPEROR'S NEW CLOTHES

I Apochrypha……..A Note on Quantum Physics.

♦♦♦♦

PREFACE

This is a second collected journalism compendium, this time featuring not just articles from Yorkshire, but with a wider scope.

Those familiar with my earlier work/ eBook, Notes from a Big County, will recognise the eclectic style; but this time the breadth of features is much wider, and not just connected to the Broad Acres.

I hope you enjoy as much as *Notes from a Big County;* all the articles enclosed have been published in the local or national press between 2006-11.

Yet again, I'm indebted to various contributors and academics, friends for their thoughts contributions and comments, and of course to my family for their on-going encouragement and support, and I acknowledge them all at the end of this collection.

Thanks also to you, dear reader, for putting up with this journalistic stroll down the haunted west wing of the mansion of knowledge.

I hope you emerge into the coffee shop and gift store of serendipity feeling a little wiser; if not, welcome to the visitor centre of the adroitly arcane.

Martin Hickes

Sept 2011

A NOTE FROM THE AUTHOR ON JOURNALISM IN THE 21ST C

Some time ago, I wrote a long piece entitled *Telegraph Road*, documenting the short history of the news and the dawn of the digital revolution.

In it, I trawled over the history of the newspaper and discussed numerous possibilities for the future of such, and journalism at large, in the new media world.

While many still believe in the long term survivability of the newspaper, events these past few months can only have fuelled the beliefs of those thinkers who are predicting a brave new world in print journalism.

Guardian News and Media bosses have told journalists that digital is now their main priority, or at least as reported in the Press Gazette.

The historic shift will see The Guardian become a "digital-first" organisation, meaning 'investment and effort is to be focused on digital rather than print'.

According to the report, digital currently contributes around £35m to £40m a year out of Guardian News and Media's £221m turnover (2009/2010 figures).

It is understood that GNM wants to double that contribution in the next five years. According to PG, last year GNM made an operating loss of £37.8m.

Print currently contributes the majority of GNM's income, but sales have been declining sharply: last month circulation of The Guardian dropped 12.5 per cent year on year to 262,937 whereas The Observer was down 13.9 per cent to 293,053.

Digital revenue and readership is growing. In April, Guardian.co.uk attracted 2.4m unique users a day according to ABC, up 31 per cent year on year.

While print is said to remain "critical" to GNM, the new strategy will see more investment in digital initiatives, such as a new US operation and mobile.

Editor Alan Rusbridger is quoted as saying: "Every newspaper is on a journey into some kind of digital future. That doesn't mean getting out of print, but it does require a greater focus of attention, imagination and resource on the various forms that digital future is likely to take."

The situation is of course not unique to the Guardian but to just about every printed newspaper and 'traditional' media outlet across the globe.

While the digital revolution and impact of the internet has had an effect on every business in Britain – look at the High Street for example – the media world has seen it as a bit of a curate's egg.

Photographers have certainly benefitted from the revolution – their costs have been sharply cut by the sunset of film and transparencies – and images from sporting events can be transmitted across the globe in a fraction of a second. [I spent more than one summer acting as a press runner for my photographer father from major sporting events 20 years ago carrying film to be developed in the ubiquitous black canisters back to darkrooms].

For journalists, while the instantaneous of the web has been a major boon to 'the news' itself, which, by its very etymology, always takes the fastest available conduit to the public consciousness, the gain is less obvious. (The 'news' is a bit like water – it always takes its swiftest route to the consumer, downhill).

In the new media torrent, some reckon/fear that newspapers COULD be left miles behind by the new techno.

Some surmise that anything which is a day old, never mind a week old, counts for little these days. A little like a panting Greek messenger arriving, carrying news of the Persian defeat at Marathon, only to find the Athenians have just installed cable.

Compared to some lickety-split techno and blogs, which allows press releases to be published worldwide within seconds of them being received by the journo/blogger, the 'traditional' press [in terms of 'the news' certainly] is in danger of becoming the wheezy -boy in the 100 metre dash alongside the Usain Bolt of news delivery.

Where the traditional press scores handsomely though, is in its broad range of experts, and the sheer depth of its coverage which can make blogs and webpages look like fly-posters on the mansion of knowledge. Magazines are a different entity altogether of course.

But is it just newspapers which might suffer? Perhaps it might be the new media outlets themselves?

The key question of course in the new age is: "Where is the money going to come from?'

Journalism is a relatively poorly paid profession, both in print and online, in the provinces as it is.

Years ago as a naive cub reporter in Bradford, to me editorial was king, and the editor the king [or queen] of the newspaper.

Advertising revenue though is of course the main revenue source – the cover price of many 'paid for' newspapers is usually a small percentage of such (and in the case of 'free' newspapers a zero factor).

Advertising managers [usually] have as much clout as the editor, if not more so; but then newspapers are 'bought to be read', (a slogan of some). Few people buy a paper solely to see if their favourite leather-seated high-back chair has gone up in price.

Ad revenues in the US as a benchmark (see my previous article) have been falling historically for a long time, and the great worry universally is that while the digital revolution is seeing some print advertisers migrate to the new format, it has been a struggle to match earlier levels.

While there is some hope for improvement, a key factor will remain the number of outlets (tv, radio, internet, broadband, print, satellite and the rest of 'the media' club) seeking to attract a finite amount of all important advertising revenue.

Some fear, in the 21st C, too little butter is being spread over too much toast. And this can only have an impact on already Dickensian-like salaries.

To some, this might all sound like scaremongering.

But for many journalists, the equivalent of Paul Revere's 'midnight ride' announcing the digital revolution has not only occurred, but many are racing to keep up with the horsetails of the already mercurial change. Many don't need the digital revolution to tell them the digital revolution is here.

For some, including ironically the watching general public, seeing journalists scurry, for once along with the rest of society, in the face of the new industrial steam roller, it might also seem to be the biggest wild-goose chase in which there is no golden pot at the end of the rainbow.

Journalism will survive, but if the ad revenues don't appear/continue, and 'pay walls' fail, paid-for journalists might not. And in the meantime, in the salmon leap of modernity, thousands of media students are still falling over themselves to vie for internships.

In the already cut-throat barber's shop of the media world, in which survivability will increasingly become key, it could be a close shave.

But it's an important concept. Imagine if a writer of the magnitude of Charles Dickens, who seemingly never stopped writing, had access to the internet and the social networks. Dickens drew a reasonable crowd at his church hall readings and oratories in Victorian England.

Given the prospect of Kindles, Google Sites/Pages and the so-called Web 2.0 social interaction technology existing in the 1800s, it's reasonable to presume there would have been no stopping him.

But then, perhaps each genius is only the product of his particular time and place.

On that thought, it's perhaps fitting that the (fictitious) Sweeney Todd lived on Fleet Street.

With web users seemingly unwilling to pay for news online, and against a backdrop of uncertain ad revenues streams, Sweeney's accomplices, Mrs Lovett and Tobias Ragg, waiting in the downstairs slurry room, might have some 'ready-made content' yet, if online readers/advertisers decide to make mincemeat of the new media world.

In trying to keep up with the voracious demands of the contemporaneousness of 'the news', has journalism (or is it about to) cut its own throat? Perhaps not.

But then again, in the fairest democracy in the world, in the absence of a written constitution (and a First Amendment), what price freedom of speech?

Journalism will survive – if it can get past the phone hacking scandal which flourishes as I write – but it what form remains to be seen. Fresh off-the-press pies anyone?

In the meantime, I hope what follows from the haunted wing of the mansion of knowledge, proves illuminating.

There are still some goldfish in the murky pool.

All good wishes to you, whereever you may be.

MH

A NOTE ON THE ARTICLES

Since this digital book covers articles dated 2006-2011, many of the people in these stories might have changed posts or moved professions. This collection is simply a gathering of articles published in the local and national press since 2006 to the current day and generally the journals were correct and contemporaneous at the time of initial publication both in print and online.

1 HERE THERE BE DRAGONS

For well over a century, monsters of sea, lake and mere have captured the imagination of many a traveller.

And while the Lake District is famous for writers of a Romantic imagination, has the tale of a mythical leviathan at the bottom of Lake Windermere become simply longer than the supposed tail on the creature itself?

Nessie of course is well known in Scotland's eponymous Loch, with over 3,000 reported 'sightings' to date, and is the subject of countless books - one in the 70s even being by the BBC's own Nicholas Witchell.

But when it comes to Windermere's own 'Bownessie' or Windy/Windie, has the story of the supposed resident of England's largest lake any foundation, or will it remain fathomless?

Stories of a supposed Nessie cousin or creature in the lake have been surfacing on and off with increased regularity in the past few years, and originally date back to the 1950s.

And only last month [Sept 2009], a group of devotees was due to set off to try to solve the mystery once and for all.

Freelance photo-journalist Linden Adams, now 38 and living in Cheshire, hit the headlines both locally and nationally in 2007 when he shot photos of an object in the lake which he saw moving in a dipping, circling movement, sighted from his vantage point at Gummers How, east of the lake, using a 70-300mm lens while walking with his wife.

Initially a sceptic, he again spotted the 'creature' some months later. And despite an acute awareness that he might be viewed as a being 'crank', he says his belief in the possibility of a creature remains strong almost three years later.

Linden, who specialises in extreme sports photography among other fields, says: "I was on Gummers How early in the morning in February 2007 looking down on the length of the lake from the vantage or view point when out walking with my wife.

"After waiting for the mist to clear off the lake, I spotted an object moving along the lake close to the peninsula beyond the Hill of Oaks caravan site which was very dark; a black dot shape leaving a wake, dipping up and down in the lake. I took the wide angle lens off my camera and switched to the longer lens.

"I then started taking the best pictures on what was not the best lens for the job but equally not wholly inadequate. I quickly checked the back of the camera and all I could see was a black dot.

"This was not before viewing the anomaly through professional binoculars for some minutes before switching to longer lens."

"I then got home, switched on the computer and downloaded the pictures from the camera which were in the RAW format, which can't be manipulated, and I realised I had got something."

The pictures, which Linden has since had independently corroborated and had forensically checked to guard against possible implied falsehood- showed the possible outline of a head, with an estimated body 12 ft protruding from the water with the overall length estimated at 65 - 70 ft.

He says:

"The head was roughly in the size of an oil barrel and I can best describe it as being akin to something like komodo dragon, or such like.

"The remarkable thing about that day was that it was one of the quietest times of the year on the lake - about 10am in the morning - and the lake was like a mirror as it often can be.

"The shape was swimming westward from the Hill of Oaks peninsula and circling in that region - in fact the geomorphology of the lake is such in that area that I wondered if it might have been feeding as it was diving, surfacing, and changing direction a great deal.

"The shape of the lake shelves deeply at that point just beyond Hill of Oaks and shelves more gently toward the western side.

"The first reported sightings of anything in the Lake I understand were in the 1950s with more being reported as the lake has quietened. With more procedures in place to maintain the harmony of the lake and the lakes, I'd be very surprised if we didn't have even more sightings in the future.

"I set up a website to spread news of my sighting and to keep people up to date with any developments, and I received many hits. Yes, some people did of course think I was a crank, but I also received many others mails of support.

"I can assure readers that I was the first among sceptics about the possibility of anything of this nature living in the lake - but I'm now convinced - and I'm not the only one."

Another possible witness to the scene was canoeist Michael Bentley from Ambleside, who was paddling in the region just ten minutes behind Mr Adams' reported sighting.

While he didn't witness the event, in March of the same year Mr Bentley claimed to have spotted the creature in the same area of lake while paddling with his partner, having seen Linden Adams' photos.

While reports of first sightings of Bownessie emerged in the 50s, one of the first people to spark Bownessie-mania was journalist and Huddersfield University media lecturer Steve Burnip, a year before before Linden Adams' sighting.

Steve says:

"In July 2006 I was on holiday at the Dower House at Wray Castle. It was the first Sunday of a week long holiday around lunchtime. I was walking along the lake with my wife and two friends and we'd walked up to Watbarrow Point which juts outs into the lake about 40ft above the water.

"Just like Linden said, the lake was very quiet because the speeding ban had come in - the previous year it would have been full of people on jet skis - and the lake was like glass.

"We were just stood chatting and I literally saw it - similar to the classic three lumps that you get in the Loch Ness pictures; I could see a head with swirling water and then a grey lump, more swirling water, and another grey lump.

"But the most remarkable thing was that it was really moving. My jaw just dropped open and I said: 'Look at that!'. My wife also saw it but very quickly it was up the lake.

"I took a picture of it on a little point and shoot digi camera I had in my pocket as an afterthought I'll be honest - by this time it had moved on towards a quarry and some trees. The pictures were pixelated but you can make out the three bumps.

"I estimated it to be at least 30 ft long. I wouldn't believe anyone else if they told me - but I saw it and I know what I saw and I reported to the tale the news editor at the Westmoreland Gazette who ran the story.

"I'm not a crank or otherwise - I'm a traditional journalist and now a lecturer used to dealing with people of all walks of life - you cover the story and you move on to the next. In fact I hesitated to report my sighting because I know how the media can pigeonhole you sometimes if you make such reports. It was the speed of the thing that really impressed me - and it was grey.

"Like most journalists, I don't like being in the news - and the only reason I ran with this was because I thought it would be interesting for my students to see how stories grow in the media. But I know what I saw.

"The story was widely reported and it interesting now how it's already passing into almost folklore."

Reports of sightings of monsters of the deep have been commonplace throughout the world for centuries.

Dr Charles Paxton, a research fellow at the school of Mathematics and Statistics, at the University of St Andrews, says:

"It would be erroneous to suggest that the report/sighting of so called monsters and associated creatures started with the Victorians - it actually started rather before that.

"The surge in sea monster reporting starts in 1817 with a series of sightings off the fishing town of Gloucester in New England, although there were reports before that.

"There was also local tourism associated with it (so I suppose you could call that "spotting").

"People would come from Boston to see the sea serpent. There is no other equivalent point in time when there was a sudden increase in sightings except for the 1930s associated with the coverage of Loch Ness.

"I say this with certainty because I have been cataloguing reports. There were reports during the Victorian period but not as far as I can tell at a rate greater than 1817-1820 in New England.

"Not many people though actually report these things. Reports of 3000+ sightings at Loch Ness which I have seen quoted to not seem to have any justification.

"As to Lake Windermere, I would say that Windermere has no real monster tradition (despite what the internet says) and, the last I heard, the number of sightings was meagre.

"Whether you regard particular sightings as evidence of unknown animals depends on the size estimation in particular photos.

"I have no expertise in that so I would like to know the estimation error associated with the procedure. Windermere has been extensively studied for over 50 years and during the war and thereafter there was a fishery for perch. Nothing strange was ever caught in any nets.

"Until someone brings this creature onto dry land in a net, we won't have proof."

Sea and lake monsters have been the staple of mythology, rumour, or local folklore for years, whose existence has largely lacked scientific support.

Many sceptics consider lake monsters to be purely exaggerations or misinterpretations of known and natural phenomena, or else suggested fabrications and hoaxes. Most lake monsters are generally believed not to exist by conventional sciences.

Misidentified sightings of seals, otters, deer, diving water birds, large fish such as giant sturgeons, logs, mirages and seiches (a type of standing wave), light distortion, crossing boat wakes, or unusual wave patterns have all been proposed to explain specific reports.

Alan Mumford, of lakedistrictboatcharter.co.uk, who runs corporate and private charters on the lake aboard a luxury Sealine T50 motorboat from Windermere Marina Village, is open minded about Bownessie.

He says:

"When out on the lake it's possible to see all sorts of distortions in the water, from strange current eddies to other odd swirls and wakes.

"I'm intrigued by the whole idea and it certainly captures the imagination of our clients. For a period we ran a special Bownessie tour on board the boat but it was unfortunately undersubscribed so we had to end it.

"I'm open minded about the idea of their being a monster in Windermere."

Alan, along with an ITV tv film crew, psychic Dean Maynard; Lake District hotelier Thomas Noblett and Linden Adams, and other enthusiasts, headed out on an exploratory cruise of the lake on September 19/20 in a bid to identify a creature on board 'Mistress'.

It is understood the documentary will be broadcast later in 2009/10.

Thomas Noblett, managing director of the Langdale Chase Hotel, which abuts the lake, who is training to make a Channel swim , was shocked when what he presumed to be Bownessie brushed past him while swimming in the Lake.

He says:

"I'm a keen swimmer and am in training to make a Channel swim. I regularly swim in the early morning in Windermere, with the hotel manager Andrew Tighe here in the timing boat, either down the length of the lake or across to Wray Castle and back again.

"On this occasion in July, again the lake was absolutely like a mirror. I was swimming alongside the boat, generally 'switched off' thinking about my stroke, and I suddenly felt something - I was lifted by a 3ft wave - a bow wave heading at speed which passed me - and then a second one after I had stopped swimming.

"We were the only ones disturbing the water because it was like a mill pond.

"I turned to Andrew and said: 'What was that?' and he confirmed there was no other craft on the lake that could have made that bow wave. We then saw the triangle of the wake of something below the surface ahead, moving at speed away from us. And because it was so flat, this bow wave went right to the shore of Windermere about 200m away.

"I know the lake well obviously and used to have no fear of the it - but now I have doubts. In fact I don't swim towards Wray Castle anymore as it gives me the hee-bee-gee-bees. When we came back in that day we were a little bit shocked and startled, and my sous-chef said there had been reports on Lakeland radio of a monster in the lake. I'm more than open minded about the whole thing now."

Sailor Gordon Clements, a boat owner on the lake and a sailor, from Finsthwaite, for more than 35 years on Windermere, says:

"I've been sailing on this lake for a long time and while I've seen many a rogue wave which can seem to come out of nowhere, I think reports of any monsters are unfounded."

This latest expedition might be unsuccessful, but in the romantic tradition of the English Lakes, as the mists of autumn and winter settle on the lake in the still of the quiet season, who can be sure what lies beneath?

ENDS

* In the horror novel The Pike (1982) by Cliff Twemlow a 12-foot (3.7 m) long pike in Windermere goes on a killing spree, and the consequence is a boom in the Lake's tourist trade.

* Windermere is one of a very few lakes in Britain which has a perceptible tide.

Windermere is a ribbon lake, formed thousands of years ago during the last Ice Age via the action of glaciation.

* It reaches a depth of over 220 feet (around 70 m) near its northern end. The main fish in the lake are trout, char, pike, and perch. The River Leven is it main link to the sea, albeit via a series of estuaries and weirs.

2 THE PRINCESS OF FINSTHWAITE

DEEP within the folds of the Lake District, in the south corner of a yard whose church chimes sweetly towards the softer fells, lies an unassuming grave of a 'forgotten princess'.

Beneath a small, white stone cross, a little battered and lichen covered through the passage of years, if legend is to be believed, rest the earthly remains of a princess of the royal Stuart line, the daughter of an outcast prince, himself son of an outcast king.

Enigmatically, the epitaph which graces the simple cross of the young girl reads 'Behold, Thy King Cometh'.

The haunting story of the girl, Clementina Johannes Sobieski Douglass, alleged daughter of Charles Edward Stuart, the Young Pretender or Bonnie Prince Charlie, has persisted in Cumbria for more than two hundred years, and has spawned rumour, counter-rumour and wild allegations, involving, at their most extreme, the supposed exhumation of the 'princess'. In 1715, James Stuart, son of the deposed Catholic

James II, attempted an abortive invasion of England via Scotland.

Ten years later, James married Princess Maria Clementina Sobieska, granddaughter of King John III, or Johannes, of Poland, and moved to Rome where the Pope recognised him as Britain's rightful king. In 1745 his son, Bonnie Prince Charlie led an uprising against George II, taking Edinburgh in the September of that year.

While staying at Bannockburn House, after retreating from defeat in Carlisle, he had the 'flu and was nursed back to health by Clementina Walkenshawe, the daughter of a prominent Jacobite – John Walkenshawe.

And it was then, according to legend, that the Prince had an affair with Clementina – long before Flora Macdonald; and Clementina bore him a child, the future 'Princess of Finsthwaite'. Some years later, a little girl came to the village of Finsthwaite. Her name was Clementina Johannes Sobieski Douglass.

The first name was that of her supposed mother, the second and third names those of the Prince's Polish family connections, and Douglass was a frequent alias used by the Prince when in hiding.

What is known for certain is that on 28 April 1770, the young woman was a witness to the will of Edward Taylor, of Waterside, and she used the name Clementina Douglass. She died, at the age of twenty-four, and was buried in the southern side of Finsthwaite churchyard on 16 May 1771, beneath the enigmatic headstone. The grave was put up only ninety years ago and was inspired by nothing firmer than a belief about who she was.

However, according to a note dated 1959 by the Rev R W Pedder of Finsthwaite House, then vicar of the parish, the original grave of the princess was dug up when the old church was being demolished.

Historian Janet Martin, a Finsthwaite resident, in her exhaustive and excellent paper The Finsthwaite Princess: The Making of a Myth, recounts that the earliest written accounts of the princess seem to be those of Richard Pedder, of Finsthwaite House, who wrote in 1870: "Clementina Johannes Sobieski Douglass lodged at Waterside house from time to time.

She was quite 'a grand lady' according to a report, and who she was and where she came from nothing was ever known except she was intimate with the Backhouses with whom she lodged."

In 1719, a medallion was struck to celebrate the marriage of 'James III', the Old Pretender, and Princess Maria Clementina Sobieski of Poland, and such a medal came into the possession of Canon Charles Gale Townley, of Staveley in Cartmel, in 1913. The medal is said to have come into the family at the bequest of the Finsthwaite princess herself, via a friend Jane Penny, who later inherited Jolliver Tree house.

Tom Cross, in his pamphlet A Lakeland Princess (1945) states that at Waterside, within a moulded over mantle, lay the initials CRA, which he thought 'probably stood for Charles, Roi Angleterre'. Ms Martin, however, suggests the solution is more straightforward, and relates to a Christopher

Robinson and his wife Agnes who lived at Waterside in the early 1700s.

Perhaps the most remarkable suggestion regarding the princess is the rumour that, in the 1970s, a story began to circulate the public houses in nearby Barrow that in the 1940s the Home Office sought the exhumation of her grave to stop possible Nazi relic hunters should an invasion occur.

Not surprisingly, today, the Home Office has no record of such an event.

Ms Martin says the truth about the princess, although never certain, is probably much more mundane. "It seems impossible that a daughter of the Pretender could have been hidden from the British Government in the eighteenth century. I can only surmise that her father was James Douglas who had been a soldier in the army of the Young Pretender, a committed Jacobite who had given his daughter her highly suggestive names.

"After the failure of the 1745 rebellion, such men were to a great extent an embarrassment to their country and a quiet life in Furness and the Lakes might have been attractive.

"That the 'princess' was witness to Edward Taylor's will argues that she was then over twenty-one years of age and of sound mind. She signed her own name, Clementina Douglass, as did James Douglass who was probably her father, but possibly her brother, uncle or cousin, who left Finsthwaite after she died."

To this day, a lone piper occasionally walks the churchyard at Finsthwaite, and a white cockade – a Jacobite symbol – is still left by devotees at the grave on significant anniversaries.

But while the Stuart line has passed into the history books, in one small corner of the home of the Lakeland Romantics, in the poetic imagination at least, a princess still lies at peace, waiting to be reunited with her long-lost father, and would-be king.

3 ANTARCTICA IN FOCUS

CAN THE OZONE HOLE 'SAVE' ANTARCTICA FROM GLOBAL WARMING?

Perhaps surprisingly to many, 2010 marks the 25th anniversary of the discovery of the hole in the ozone layer above Antarctic.

Even more extraordinarily perhaps, in the midst of so-called 'climate-gate', scientists are for the first time beginning to understand how the huge gape above Antarctica might actually be shielding the frozen continent from global warming.

As the furore continues across the globe as to whether global warming does or doesn't exist, at the base of the world, scientists are in no doubt as to what is going on.

Experts have just this month (Dec 1, 2010) published an exhaustive review of the dynamic eco-system of Antarctica – and have come to the perhaps startling conclusion that the infamous hole might actually be 'protecting' the unique Antarctic environment, among a raft of other key findings.

The Antarctic Climate Change and the Environment (ACCE) is a major report collating all present knowledge on the past and possible future changes in the physical environment of Antarctica and the Southern Ocean.

Preparation of the report was led by the SCAR Antarctica and the Global Climate System (AGCS) groups with input from other major external groups and experts.

Key among the findings is the extent to which the huge ozone hole – well documented since 1985 – might actually be protecting the fragile frozen environment rather than aiding its destruction.

Scientists have also discovered an array of previously unknown but linked environmental effects are at play on the planet's coldest landmass.

Dr. Colin Summerhayes, Executive Director of the Scientific Committee on Antarctic Research (SCAR) says:

"Antarctica is an unrivalled source of information about our planet.

"This review describes what we know now and illustrates how human activity is driving rapid climate change.

"By integrating this multidisciplinary evidence into a single source, we are helping scientists and policy makers understand the distinction between environmental changes linked to the Earth's natural cycles, and those that are human induced.

"The work is particularly important because it puts Antarctic climate change into context and reveals the impact on the rest of the planet."

Professor John Turner of British Antarctic Survey is the lead editor of the review.

He says:

"For me the most astonishing evidence is the way that one man-made environmental impact — the ozone hole — has shielded most of Antarctica from another — global warming. Understanding the complexities surrounding these issues is a challenge for scientists — and communicating these in a meaningful way to society and to policymakers is essential.

"There is no doubt that our world is changing and human activity is accelerating global change. This review is a major step forward in making sure that the latest and best evidence is available in one place.

"It sets the scene for future Antarctic Research and provides the knowledge that we all need to help us live with environmental change.

"This review draws together important information from different scientific disciplines (such as meteorology, glaciology and biology) and many aspects of the global climate system."

Prof Turner adds:

"The ozone hole has delayed the impact of greenhouse gas increases on the climate of the continent.

"Consequently south polar winds (the polar vortex) have intensified and affected Antarctic weather patterns, while westerly winds over the Southern Ocean that surrounds Antarctica have increased.

"The upshot is the stronger winds have effectively isolated Antarctica from the warming elsewhere on the planet.

"As a result during the past 30 years, there has been little change in surface temperature over much of the vast Antarctic continent, although West Antarctica has warmed slightly.

"An important exception is the eastern coast of the Antarctic Peninsula, which has seen rapid summer warming. This warming is caused by stronger westerly winds bringing warm, wet air into the region from the ocean."

While the ozone hole and global warming were thought to be crucially linked in past, scientists have been puzzling for years quite how exactly this was so.

It's generally accepted that reductions of up to 70% in the ozone layer first observed and first reported in 1985 are continuing.

The hole is in the stratosphere, which has seen ozone levels historically drop to as low as 33% of their pre-1975 values.

It occurs during the Antarctic spring, from September to early December, as strong westerly winds start to circulate around the continent and create an atmospheric container.

Within this so-called polar vortex, over 50% of the lower stratospheric ozone is destroyed annually.

Since 1981, the United Nations Environment Programme has sponsored a series of reports on scientific assessment of ozone depletion.

Prof Turner says:

"The Montreal Protocol is an international agreement that has phased out production of CFCs, Halons, and some other organic chlorides and bromides, collectively referred to as Ozone Depleting Substances (ODSs).

"Because of its success, the amounts of ODSs in the stratosphere are now starting to decrease. However, there is as yet no convincing sign of any reduction in the size or depth of the ozone hole, although the sustained increases up the 1990s have not continued.

"Great advances have been made in recent years into our understanding of Antarctic climate and environmental change. We now know that the climate system of the high southern latitudes is very complex and that there is variability on a range of time scales.

"We also know that changes in the atmospheric and oceanic circulation around Antarctica, and the volume of the ice sheets, interact and influence climate at a global scale.

"Although a great deal of data is now available with which to investigate change – both in the past and over the next century, there are still major gaps in our knowledge and many areas where we require additional instrumental data gathering and model development.

"The CFCs that are responsible for the ozone hole have a long lifetime in the atmosphere and our best estimate is that it will be 2060-2070 before stratospheric ozone concentrations above the Antarctic recover to pre-ozone hole levels."

The Scientific Committee on Antarctic Research (SCAR) is the main body dealing with the international co-ordination of scientific research in Antarctica and the Southern Ocean.

The British Antarctic Survey (BAS), a component of the Natural Environment Research Council, delivers world-leading interdisciplinary research in the Polar Regions. Its skilled science and support staff based in Cambridge, Antarctica and the Arctic.

Key findings of the report:

• Long-term monitoring reveals that the ozone hole has delayed the impact of greenhouse gas increases on Antarctica's climate.

• The largest ocean current on Earth (the Antarctic Circumpolar Current) has warmed faster than the global ocean as a whole.

- Rapid warming has been seen along the western Antarctic Peninsula, resulting in expansion of plant, animal and microbial communities in newly available land.

- The West Antarctic Ice Sheet has significantly thinned particularly around the Amundsen Sea Embayment as a result of warmer ocean temperatures.

- Since 1980 there has been a 10% increase in Antarctic sea ice extent, particularly in the Ross Sea region, as a result of the stronger winds around the continent (due to the ozone hole).

- Ice core research shows that atmospheric concentrations of CO_2 are at higher levels than experienced in the last 800,000 years and are increasing at rates unlikely to have been seen in the (geologically) recent past.

- Over this century the ozone hole is expected to heal, allowing the full effects of greenhouse gas increases to be felt across the Antarctic.

- The predicted future warming of about 3°C across the continent is not enough to melt the main ice sheet and an increase in snowfall should offset sea level rise by a few centimetres.

4 REALITY AIN'T WHAT IT USED TO BE

In the current vogue for 'Big Picture' explanations in the smarter corners of bookstores, either real or virtual, the occasional goldfish in the murky pool arises.

This is thankfully so with Decoding Reality, (OUP £16.99) Prof Vlatko Vedral's major new literary big toe in the oceanic milieu of otherwise cosmic near-incomprehensibility.

Vedral, erstwhile of the University of Leeds and now at Oxford, ponders that the nature of reality might be even more complex than anyone has ever considered before, with the exotic property of quantum 'information; lying at its heart. And it's spectacular stuff even for the lay reader.

Prof Vedral suggests while light, gravity, and the 'classical' understandings of Einstein and Newton, as well as the 'random' world of quantum physics continue to be the twin theoretical headlights shining into void, 'quantum information' might be science's new 'high beam'.

Taking a leaf out of the book of the brilliant Italian journalist and semiologist Italo Calvino, he suggests the secrets of the 'information'-grounded universe have been effectively unfolding since the Big Bang in the same discreet fashion in which a dealer deals cards which have initially no meaning to the recipients around the table. The secrets of the infinite, it seems are all a question of interpretation.

Vedral says:

"'Information may seem a mundane word – bringing to mind rows of numbers, vast databases etc – but information is the most profound concept in modern science. The Universe and everything in it can be understood in terms of 'information.'

"I'm trying to present the most up to date scientific picture of our universe, and grapple with the notion of what fundamentally defines our reality. As strange as it may sound, I'm trying to impress….that it is quantum information rather than energy or matter or anything else you can think of, that is the most fundamental entity in the universe.

Prof Vedral speaks of the possible use of teleportation in the future, and the use of quantum cryptography, already in use today, which might appeal to those of a Dan Brown mind-set.

He says: "The most profound question humans can ask and facing science today is the nature of reality. Why is there 'anything' out there in the first place – surely 'nothing' would be the simplest state to have? Quantum physics and information theory hold the answer I believe.

'As a child I remember feeling a little lost by rules I was required to learn verbatim and just imagined them to be a magician's trick, something my teacher pulled out of the hat.

'Further along in life, these tricks don't seem so intimidating…[and then later] we are in a position to speculate…whether there is a master book of magic which governs them all.

'Whatever walk of life you come from, the question remains the same – is the reality we see around us made up from a seemingly random collection of rules and events or is there a common underlying thread?

'Postulating a supernatural being does not really help explain reality since we only displace the question of the origins of reality to explaining the origins of the supernatural being.

'If you think scientists might have vastly more insightful understanding of the universe compared to that of major religions, then you'd better think again.

'From the point of view explaining why there is a reality and where it ultimately comes from, being religious or not makes absolutely no difference – we all end up with the same tricky question.'

The book's startling epilogue is an absolute must read with profound implications for our existence and perceptions of reality.

Certainly Decoding Reality stands alongside The Void, the stable mate from fellow Oxford physics luminary Prof Frank Close.

In a new information age, whether scientific popularists are the prestidigitators of today, or the new alchemists of our pseudo understanding, perhaps remains open to question.

As with most things, in the end, is seems, all will be revealed.

Too much information? Not in this case.

ENDS

◦Vlatko Vedral studied undergraduate theoretical physics at Imperial College London, where he also received a PhD for his work on 'Quantum Information Theory of Entanglement'.

◦He has written for popular science journals and major daily newspapers, as well as doing extensive radio programmes and television interviews.

5 MASTERS OF THE UNIVERSE

THE ROARING success of *The King's Speech* across the globe perhaps underlines audiences' love for a storyline which, on first hearing of such, might sound slightly prosaic, but which, when realised on screen, combines all the passion, angst and emotional intensity of the very best of historical dramas.

In light of such, those screenplay writers looking for inspiration from, perhaps, an unlikely source could do well to turn to science writer Jim Baggott's absorbing 'The Quantum Story' (OUP £16.99).

The arcane world of particle physics – not least quantum physics – can on the face of it, seem to be an exceptionally dry one.

Often the wallflower at the disco of life, to many, quantum physics, has suffered a little in the general public domain thanks to its nigh-on mind-boggling incomprehensibility.

But its great paradox, as with Mr Baggott's absorbing tour de force, is that, to this day, in its sheer esotericism, lies its infinite depth and appeal.

Never mind Superman, the real masters of the universe lie beneath the Clark Kent-like alter egos of particle physicists.

Mr Baggott's marvellous work has all the properties of a quark itself – charm, intensity, excitement, strangeness, dynamic colour, as well as a story of the curious emotional bi-poles of dizzy euphoria and crushing despair felt by the greatest minds on the planet in the search for the basic answers to what makes the universe tick.

The star of the show is the enigmatic theory itself, which defies easy explanation, but which, quite simply, is probably the most tantalising theory mankind has ever chanced to formulate.

But like the very best protagonist, its greater attraction, and that of the book, is that it also gives us a glimpse of the true heart of darkness which seems to underpin the nature of 'reality' itself on the very small level.

Most A-level school leavers know of Newton and Einstein and their attempts to describe the harmony of the movements of the so-called classical, large scale world; the motion of things, including the planets, the nature of space and time, light; the four fundamental forces of Nature: gravity, electromagnetism and the nuclear forces which hold atoms together.

Einstein built on Newton's theories in the early 20th C with his special and general theory of relativity, which to many at the time (and still to this day) seemed to neatly sum up - or at least give a very good working approximation - as to how the known universe works.

At the start of the century, a lot of scientists - empiricists to the end - perhaps had reason to feel ever so slightly self-satisfied with themselves that the universe could not only seemingly be reckoned by science, but that the nature of things might be ultimately 'knowable'.

Then enter, like the best pantomime villain, quantum theory, which in the early years of the century, threw a (Schrodinger's) cat among the pigeons of scientific certainty.

Some scientists happened to notice that, on the very small level, things — specifically the very small elements of matter — didn't behave as they perhaps should.

When it was found in 1900 by Max Planck that wave energy could be described as consisting of small packets or quanta, Albert Einstein and others further developed this idea to show that an electromagnetic wave such as light could be described as a particle - later called the photon.

But in trying to measure the position of very small particles, it seemed a fundamental uncertainty lie at the heart of the things.

Worryingly, scientists could not accurately pinpoint the position of the very smallest of the building blocks of existence with absolute certainty.

In fact, it seemed at the heart of the matter, particles could at best be described as only having a probability of existing in a certain place or not.

And in the precise world of physics, chance was the equivalent of a hair in the cosmic vichyssoise.

Totally counter-intuitively, some particles seemed to have the impossible ability to be in two places at the same time.

Over the course of a few years at the dawn of the 20th C, the greatest minds on the planet began to struggle with the concept that on the large scale, things seemed to operate within well-defined parameters and with a certain beauty; but on the scale of the very small, much seemed disconcertingly chaotic and totally unpredictable.

Mr Baggott eloquently describes how Einstein famously initially questioned quantum theory, with his famous quote: "God Does Not Play Dice…..". And how, despite various attempts to debunk quantum theory by many, the theory seems unerringly accurate.

In his preface, Mr Baggott says: " 'The last century was defined by physics. From the minds of the world's leading physicists, there flowed a river of ideas that would transport mankind to the pinnacle of wonder and to the very depths of despair.

'This was a century which began with the certainties of absolute knowledge, and ended with the knowledge of absolute uncertainty. It was a century in which physicists developed theories that would deny us the possibility that we can never properly comprehend the nature of physical reality.

'Almost everything we think we know about the nature of the world comes from one theory of physics [quantum theory]. ..

'But this success has come at a price…for it has at the same time completely undermined our ability to make sense of the world at the level of its most fundamental constituents.

'Niels Bohr claimed that anyone who was not shocked by the theory has not understood it. The charismatic American physicist Richard Feynman went further: he claimed that nobody understands it.

'[It] is at once mathematically challenging, maddeningly bizarre, and breathtakingly beautiful…

'While nobody really understands how quantum theory actually works, the rules of its application are unquestioned and the accuracy of its predictions are unsurpassed in the history of science…..' "

And if that isn't worth £16.99, or indeed a draft Hollywood screenplay, perhaps nothing in this increasingly chaotic world is.

6 SETTING SAIL FOR THE STARS

IT might look like something out of one of the new Star Wars films, but thanks to the latest technology, space scientists have plans to set sail for the stars – quite literally.

NASA and The Planetary Society are gearing up for three pioneering missions for the revolutionary new Light-Sail craft, namely Light-Sail 1, 2 and 3, which will push the boundaries of space travel.

The new craft – if given the green light next year – will deploy a sail which will use the impact of photons from sunlight and lasers against a special gigantic space sail to accelerate the probe into orbit and possibly to the stars.

Scientists say it is a major leap forward for both a clean and cheap means of space propulsion.

Sunlight, rather than the solar wind, will power the craft, and tiny lasers could kick in when the sun's rays are too weak to propel the probe. Each method uses photons to bombard a huge solar sail, powering the craft through space.

The new solar sail project, boosted by a one-million-dollar anonymous donation, is the beginning of an innovative program that could see the launch of three separate space-sailing craft over the course of several years.

A spokesman for the Planetary Society, which is in talks with NASA over future mission plans, says:

"Solar sail propulsion is simple in concept. Light photons bounce onto a mirror-like aluminium Mylar sail. As each photon hits, its momentum is transmitted to the spacecraft.

"Photons have no mass but lots of energy, so a solar sail space probe requires no on-board fuel. The force acts continuously, meaning a solar sail can eventually reach speeds five to ten times greater than any chemical rocket.

"Russia, the U.S. and the European Space Agency all started solar sail missions and technology programs but cut them back when money got tight. Japan, we are happy to say, is now moving ahead to develop an innovative solar sail and solar-powered ion drive hybrid.

"Yet solar sail propulsion remains largely neglected. That's why the Society has long championed efforts to prove its value.

"We partnered with Cosmos Studios on the far-sighted Cosmos 1 solar sail project. But technology has advanced enormously since then. We can do more in a fraction of the size, with a fraction of the weight and at a fraction of the cost. This has led us to re-think everything…and what we've arrived at is far more advanced, and ultimately far more valuable.

"This technology also opens up many new possibilities for piggyback launching into Earth orbit, which is desperately needed since launch vehicles have been a hindrance preventing solar sail flight. We're considering several launch possibilities and will select the most reliable one that matches our schedule and final orbit choice best."

So how does it work?

When the light from the Sun reflects off the surface of the solar sail, the energy and momentum of light particles known as "photons" are transferred to the sail.

This gives the sail a "push" that accelerates it through space.

Although the acceleration is very slight, it is also continuous, unlike rockets using chemical engines that fire until the spacecraft reaches a cruising speed, when they are turned off to conserve fuel.

A solar sail can accelerate constantly and reach very high speeds in a relatively short time.

The direction of the push is controlled by the angle of the sail with respect to the Sun, adding to or subtracting from the orbital velocity.

The great advantage of a solar sail is that it requires 'no fuel'.

A solar sail spacecraft can, in time, move the spacecraft even faster than a chemical rocket. For a round trip to another planet and back, solar sails have great advantages since they don't need to carry fuel for the return leg.

The sails are made of aluminium-coated, reinforced Mylar about 1/4 the thickness of a bin liner. The sail must be as light as possible to maximize the acceleration.

The real advantage of solar sailing is that, unlike a chemical rocket that applies a lot of thrust for a very short time, sunlight hitting the sail applies thrust continuously.

In 100 days, a sail-propelled craft could reach 14,000 kilometres per hour. In just three years, a solar sail could reach over 150,000 miles per hour.

At that speed, the craft could reach Pluto in less than five years.

NASA announced this week that the Planetary Society's LightSail-1 solar sail mission is on their short list for upcoming launch opportunities. The missions selected are Cubesats destined for piggyback launches as part of NASA's CubeSat Launch Initiative.

"This is great news," said Louis Friedman, Program Director for LightSail-1. "Our spacecraft will be ready this summer, and we are hoping for the earliest launch possible."

LightSail-1 will have four triangular sails, arranged in a diamond shape resembling a giant kite.

It will be placed in an orbit over 800 kilometres above Earth, high enough to escape the drag of Earth's uppermost atmosphere.

At that altitude the spacecraft will be subject only to the force of gravity keeping it in orbit and the pressure of sunlight on its sails increasing the orbital energy.

The Planetary Society team say solar sails can be used to boost or decrease the orbits of spacecraft, hold a spacecraft in position to monitor the Sun for solar storms, provide stable Earth observation platforms, travel between the planets within our solar system, and someday take us to worlds around other stars.

* Writers and visionaries have imagined 'clipper-ships' to the stars and planets for years.

* If the early missions are given the green light and are successful, the third Light-Sail-3 craft when launched, could be parked at a special balanced gravity point in space between the earth and the Sun, called a Lagrange point, where is could act as a solar weather station feeding data back to earth.

7. BARACK OBAMA AND THE ART OF RHETORIC

Few people can claim to have an insight into the psyche of US presidents, but for one Stateside-born Sheffield academic, President Barack Obama is always on his mind.

Sheffield University's Dr James Fitzmaurice, who attended the prestigious and profoundly liberal arts college Occidental College – the alma mater of the likes of the then 'Barry' Obama, actor Ben Affleck, and director Terry Gilliam, says the 'lotus-eating' culture of one of the US's most expensive and highly regarded institutions has more than moulded the laid-back image of the most 'powerful man in the world'.

Now Dr Fitzmaurice, from Sheffield University's English department, and a distinguished alumnus of 'Oxy' - as it is affectionately known among US graduates – hopes to entice Yorkshire folk on a tour, in spirit at least, of 'Obama-land.'

His latest work – 'Memories of Obamaland' - is an affectionate and academically astute reflection on the laid-back but privileged world of Occidental, and the shaping of presidential personality.

Dr Fitzmaurice, a semi-retired professor from the Northern Arizona University, but a Sheffield resident since 2006 says:

"There's no doubt that Barack – or 'Barry' Obama as he was known at Occidental - is one of the most charismatic figures of the 21 century.

"But I wonder how many people – especially in Britain - recognise the influence that his college years might have had on - as he has been styled - the first presidential 'king of cool'.

"As an American, I was lucky enough to attend Occidental a few years ahead of Barack, and had first hand experience of the totally unique atmosphere which shaped his 'artsy skills' - and his absolute skill with language and rhetoric.

"If you refer to Occidental as fostering a culture of 'being cool' and seeming to be 'effortless' in its outlook and as 'not being excitable' – both then and now – then that would be a pretty good assessment not only of the college, but I think hence of Obama's personality.

"As an example, in his recent autobiography, Obama doesn't rise to the bait when someone makes a remark which might have been construed as being inflammatory – he just takes it easy, …and that was the way things were at Occidental both when I was there, when he was there, and now. I've just return from there recently after a vacation.

"I have a daughter who went to Occidental after Obama and I have a sense from her and from the academics I talk to when I go home, that it is very much the same type of place."

Occidental is noted for its combination of rigorous academic programs, a small yet diverse student body and its liberal arts culture to this day.

Located not far from the West Coast beaches, the college, whose name nominally means 'western', exhibits classical architectural gravitas alongside acumen of equal measure.

Barack Obama is usually described as being a graduate of Columbia University, where he earned his bachelor's degree, and later of Harvard Law School.

But he began his undergraduate education at Occidental, essentially his freshman years at the 2000-strong institute in the Eagle Rock neighbourhood of Los Angeles.

Despite the fact that Obama transferred from Occidental, he was a good athlete who helped the JV Tigers basketball team to an undefeated season.

He graduated magna cum laude from Harvard Law School some years later, and the rest is history.

Jim, a graduate from Occidental in 1965 says:

"'Oxy' was both a 'lefty' American liberal arts college of the usual sort and at the same time significantly more committed to racial equality in 1979 certainly than others of its ilk.

"A lot of these colleges have grown much larger over the years, but Occidental has remained pretty much the same. 'Cool' is what we were all trying to be – it was our 'watchword if you like.

"I was born in California and went there to study Comparative Literature - it was then very much a 'family' college – (my mother had gone there). I'm now a semi-retired professor of English living and teaching in Sheffield, and for a long time resident in Arizona.

"Oxy is still a Presbyterian school, but it broke from 'control' with the Presbyterian Church, and like many other American church-related schools which began as 'missionary' training grounds, became an independent liberal arts college. In fact, it was probably even a little more 'free-thinking' in its ethos than some others, even all the way back to the 1930s.

"It is still much sought after – being in what many Americans view as being the 'second tier' after the traditional, well known 'Ivy League' colleges such as Princeton and Yale.

"But it's still very much a family school in that people's parents and grandparents went there, with an intake from predominantly the state of California and the NW/Seattle area etc.

"Readers of Obama's autobiography sometimes surmise Occidental was his alma mater – the 'mother of his soul' – whereas Columbia was the mother of his 'vita', and I think he did want to plump up his resume with the Ivy League institution.

"Barack Obama is admired in the American press for his willingness to "do his homework"; he is smart and disciplined, tough minded and savvy.

"But his years of poetry writing which he gave up or toned down when he left laid-back Los Angeles and took up residence in no-nonsense New York are also significant.

"If the story of the rejection of his 'lotus eating days' at Oxy, to those who know their Shakespeare, is a little like Prince Hal's rejection of the crew from the Boar's Head Tavern, it should come as no surprise.

"His autobiography, Dreams from My Father, owes a large debt to modes of fiction and to his time at Oxy. Its author has by no means rejected the world of art and literature.

"And it's also perhaps significant that his inauguration, unlike those of the Bushes and Reagan, included a poetry reading. Elizabeth Alexander, poet and playwright, read a set of verses composed for the occasion, even as Robert Frost read newly-written poetry for the inauguration of John F. Kennedy.

"As a master of rhetoric – the old Greek/Roman art of persuasive public speaking – Obama has few rivals – and I think his Occidental years hold the key.

"It's a carefully-sculpted garden of earthy and intellectual delights tucked away in the lower middle class and ethnically diverse Eagle Rock district of Los Angeles."
Occidental College was founded on April 20, 1887, by a group of Presbyterian clergy and laymen.

The college's first term began a year later with 27 men and 13 women students, and tuition of $50 a year. Full all-in fees now can be as much as $25,000 per year.

Despite a strong Presbyterian presence on its campus, Occidental cut ties to the church in 1910.

In 1912, trustees decided to convert Oxy into an all-men's institution. However, students protested, and the idea was abandoned.

Dr Fitzmaurice, whose current study, 'Memories of Obamaland' aims to encapsulate the heady atmosphere and richness of language enshrined by his alma mater, says California also has wealth beyond academia.

He says:
"California is synonymous with a West Coast intelligentsia and I return as often as I can, but it also has an immense geographical appeal, as anyone from Britain who has been there will have discovered.

"Apart from the usual student locales, another popular haunt Obama would know is the Cal Tech and JPL hangout Burger Continental. JPL people run the Mars rovers and are usually very colourful. That place does a wild Armenian burger.

"Obama's style is very non-confrontational, polished and persuasive through eloquence. His style is his own, and there's no comparison with somebody like George W Bush, who was a 'malaprop' for much of the time and who didn't know what many words meant – but used them anyway!"

"But it's interesting that Bush was descended from what we call 'old East Coast' money and the 'Establishment'; although Obama is very much the 'self-made man'. Again he 'seems' to have done this 'effortlessly'.

"British politics might be mired in expenses scandals currently which I sense is causing a real apathy among the British public, but there is, at least, still a degree of political 'belief' or conviction in the US.

"We have scandals in America of a different sort - and perhaps Richard Nixon held the patent on those, but certainly all parties are now looking at how they operate, especially the Republicans. Perhaps they should take a leaf of out Occidental - and Obama's - 'cool' approach…? We'll just have to wait and see.

"In the meantime, I love Yorkshire and Sheffield…it's kind of cool!"

• Jim Fitzmaurice, Northern Arizona University Emeritus Professor of English, is Director of Distance Learning for the School of English at the University of Sheffield. He is convenor of Sheffield's online MA in English.

8 THE GHOST OF DICKENS'S YORKSHIRE PAST?

FOR MANY, at the festive season, Charles Dickens' annual favourite A Christmas Carol has become the literary equivalent of turkey with all the trimmings.

The tale of Scrooge and his ghostly visitors on Christmas Eve has sent a chill down the spine of readers since first appearing in print in 1843.

And while the counting houses of London and the squalor of Victorian England are thought to have provided the imaginative spark for Dickens' classic short novel, new evidence suggests he was haunted by Yorkshire as the inspiration for the tale.

Enthusiasts now argue Malton, in North Yorkshire, perhaps surprisingly, is the spiritual home of the much-loved characters Marley, Bob Cratchit, Scrooge and Tiny Tim among others.

The story was first published on 19 December 1843 and quickly met with commercial and critical acclaim.

Dickens was born in Portsmouth, Hampshire, but lived largely in London and Kent as a boy, enjoying a happy childhood, though with a dark episode of poverty and factory labour.

Many Dickensians have always thought the south of England to be the inspiration for the classic, but Malcolm Chalk, of the Charles Dickens (Malton) Society, says when it comes to A Christmas Carol, Dickens' connection with Yorkshire has more credence.

He says:

"The town of Malton was visited often by Charles Dickens because of his long friendship with Charles Smithson, a solicitor in the town. The Smithson family had their offices on Chancery Lane in Malton and they also shared a practice in London.

"Some of the connections, although not written down, are so obvious they must be true.

"The novel A Christmas Carol wasn't actually written at Malton, but the Smithson family were told by Dickens that the office in Chancery Lane was the model for Scrooge's Office and that the midnight 'Bells' in the novel were those of St Leonard's Church on Church Hill.

"I think Dickens must have been inspired to use the Smithson building as the model for Scrooge's counting room, because it's not a big office and would be a typical solicitor's office of the day.

"Charles Dickens acted as surety for a friend of his to buy into the Smithson's London business and that's how he and Charles Smithson met and became lifelong friends. Dickens came up regularly to see him.

"And because Dickens was famous, his visits made the news!

"It is said in The Yorkshire Gazette on July 8th 1843: 'We understand that Charles Dickens Esq the admired and talented author of "Pickwick", etc is now on a visit with his lady at Easthorpe, the hospitable abode of Charles Smithson Esq Solicitor, Malton, and that he has visited Old Malton Abbey and other remarkable places in the vicinity.'

"When he was in Malton, Dickens used to stay with Smithson at Easthorpe Hall and then at the Abbey house, and he was inspired by the town, by the people in it and by the surrounding area.

"Unfortunately in 1844 Charles Smithson died early like his brothers, he was only 39. He died without leaving a will, but he became one of Dickens' characters too. The family were told he was Mr Spenlow of Spenlow and Jorkins in David Copperfield.

"Dickens attended the funeral at Old Malton. He left York by fast carriage at 7.00 am on 5th April and arrived in Malton just in time for the funeral at 9.30 am.

"Now it's time Malton made more of this great literary connection....."

Over time, Dickens met other people connected with Smithson and Yorkshire. John Brodie in Nicholas Nickleby, is allegedly modelled on Richard Barnes, a Barnard Castle attorney.

Dickens also wrote part of Martin Chuzzlewit while staying in Yorkshire, and it's widely believed he entertained an audience at Malton's Saville Street's theatre (now defunct).

A Christmas Carol received immediate critical acclaim, one reviewer declaring it: 'A tale to make the reader laugh and cry—to open his hands, and open his heart to charity even toward the uncharitable [...] a dainty dish to set before a King.'"

Poet and editor Thomas Hood wrote: "If Christmas, with its ancient and hospitable customs, its social and charitable observances, were ever in danger of decay, this is the book that would give them a new lease."

'Dickens' A Christmas Carol', says Professor Francis O'Gorman from the School of English at the University of Leeds, 'remains a favourite partly because it mixes the pleasures of a ghost story—the rattling chains, the night-time visitations, the glimpses of hell—with a story of real earthly redemption and good cheer. The ghosts scare Scrooge, but more importantly they come to teach him a moral lesson about generosity and kindness. It is a tale about the affirmation of life, about the chances of doing things better'.

Prof John Bowen, from the University of York, an acknowledged expert on Dickens, adds a word of caution.

He says:

"While there is no doubt that Dickens did visit Malton – and enthusiasts can trace his visits in the great Pilgrim edition of Dickens' letters – he also visited many, many other places.

"I'm also pretty sceptical about identifying his fictional characters with real people, other than the few attested cases, such as Jane Seymour Hill as Miss Mowcher, in David Copperfield, evidence for which exists in the letters.

 "Briefly, I'm sceptical about the idea that Dickens based Marley's office on a place in Malton, although it's well known that he stayed in the town.

"A Christmas Carol is clearly set in large city, almost certainly London, and Dickens must have known many offices like Scrooge's, as he worked for several years as a lawyer's clerk."

Dickens himself returned to the tale time and again during his life to tweak the phrasing and punctuation, and capitalized on the success of the book by annually publishing other Christmas stories in 1844, 1845, 1846, and 1848.

The Chimes, The Cricket on the Hearth, The Battle of Life, and The Haunted Man and the Ghost's Bargain were all based on the pattern laid down in Carol. While the public eagerly bought the later books, the critics bludgeoned them.

By 1849, Dickens was working on David Copperfield and had neither the time nor the inclination to produce another Christmas book, though he would return to A Christmas Carol as part of his on-going popular public readings every Christmas.

Whatever the geographical truth, the minor classic, written by a man who witnessed the horrors of extreme poverty at first hand, just before the passing of the Poor Laws, remains a popular seasonal morality tale with children, parents, and curmudgeonly employers, to this day.

◦The Charles Dickens (Malton) Society has opened a Charles Dickens museum at the Chancery Lane premises and has ambitious plans to open a Dickens Experience in Malton to attract visitors over time. The society was formally started in February 2008 at a meeting of the initial eight members and now boasts a membership of over 50.

• Dickens would go on to write 15 major novels and countless short stories and articles before his death on June 9, 1870.

9 STAR OF WONDER?

For years, the wondrous image and myth of the Star of Bethlehem has vexed scholars, astronomers and religious enthusiasts alike.

Central to the story of Christmas for over 2,000 years, as well as many Christmas cards, the true identity of the "westward leading" star has remained shrouded in mystery.

But this Christmas, thanks to new technology, and perhaps a historical quirk, experts say they are closer than ever to revealing its true identity.

The revelations – using the latest computer wizardry – will be unveiled as part of a BBC documentary tonight which pinpoints the likeliest candidates for the Star – with major implications for the date of birth of Jesus.

The Bible recounts how the Magi – ancient astronomers in the pre-AD Middle East – were drawn westward by a star to the court of the Roman client king Herod, prophesying the birth of a saviour in Bethlehem.

Serious scientists – including astronomer Johannes Kepler in the 1600s – have long since dismissed the possibility of the object being a brilliant comet – the favourite theory for years.

Now, experts think the blazing star may well have been a brilliant triple planetary conjunction crucially, preceded by the movements of a significant planet such as Jupiter across the sky from the ancient skies of the east to the west in the Holy Land.

And it might just mean Jesus was born in late spring, rather than the traditional festive period.

"The latest computer programming technology allows us to see the movements in the night sky from two thousand years ago," says

James Taylor, who produced Star of Bethlehem – Behind the Myth.

"The specialist software can accurately predict the paths of the stars and planets in the future – and in the past. We can now understand the astronomical events that the wise men in the east could have witnessed.

"The on-going debate about when exactly Jesus was born and a dispute over the date of the death of Herod, means that a number of different theories are emerging from the experts using computer simulations of the ancient night skies.

"Although the birth of Christ has been taken as the start of the Christian calendar, zero BC, mistakes were made when a monk called Exiguus calculated this dating system in the 6th century.

"It has since been established that Jesus must have been born in 4BC or earlier as King Herod, who was alive when Jesus was born, is recorded as dying in the year we now call 4BC

"So astronomers are looking at astronomical events in 4, 5, 6, 7 and 8 BC in search of an identity for the Star of Bethlehem.

"At the time of Christ's birth, comets were thought to be portents of death and destruction rather than a signal of positive events. So it's highly unlikely that a comet would have inspired the wise men's epic journey. With their detailed knowledge of the night sky, these stargazing priests may have attached great importance to unusual, if not visually spectacular, astronomical events that would seem unremarkable to most people."

Leading astronomer David Hughes, emeritus professor of astronomy at the University of Sheffield, believes he can identify such an event.

He says: "In 7BC, there was a rare series of meetings between Jupiter and Saturn in the night sky. In this triple conjunction, Jupiter, the royal star, and Saturn came together in the sky three times over the course of several months. Significantly, this occurred with the constellation of Pisces in the background, which is associated with Israel.

"There is even evidence that Persian astronomers predicted the conjunction on an ancient clay tablet, now in the British

Museum. The tablet calculates solar, lunar and planetary activity for that year, and describes the conjunctions of Jupiter and Saturn in the constellation of Pisces.

"The wise men were literally that, and to draw their attention, whatever happened would have to have been something which occurred not just once every few years, but perhaps once every 800 years such as a Piscean triple conjunction."

European Space Agency astronomer Dr Mark Kidger says it would have taken more than unusual planetary movements to persuade such seasoned astronomical experts as the Magi to travel to Judea. He thinks the Magi could have seen a star entering its supernova phase – the massive surge of energy and matter would have been visible to the Magi as a new star.

He hopes future radio telescopes will be able to detect a faint bubble of expanding gas around the candidate – in the constellation of Aquila – and calculate when exactly the bubble started to expand.

But one final theory has the most surprising twist of all – Jesus may have really been born on December 25

Texan law professor and astronomer Rick Larson believes the crucial calculation of Herod's death, and therefore Jesus's birth, is inaccurate

He says: "The 4BC date is based on the writings of the historian Josephus, but every Josephus manuscript I have studied dating before 1544 is consistent with Herod having died in 1BC.

"In 2BC, Jupiter – the 'king of the planets' – met up with one of the brightest stars in the sky – Regulus, known by the Persian Magi as the 'little king' in the eastern sky.

"Nine months later, the same planet Jupiter, travelling towards the West, met up with Venus, known by the Magi as the 'mother planet'.

"The meeting of the king and mother of planets would have been highly significant – as was the timescale involved.

"To the naked eye, the planets would have seemed so close that they would have looked like one bright light in the sky."

Professor Larson believes it is this light – low down in the west of mid-June of 2BC – which prompted the Magi to travel to Jerusalem where they met Herod, who, fearing a Messianic prophecy, pointed them towards Bethlehem.

He even asserts as the Magi travelled from Jerusalem to Bethlehem, Jupiter continued to move across the sky until it reached its "retrograde stage" – a well-known astronomical quirk – when it appeared to "stand still" in the sky. He claims this happened on December 25.

If this theory is right, then the first Christmas really did occur on the day we have come to celebrate it on.

Others believe Jesus was born in late spring, and that early followers "superimposed" the celebration of his birth onto the "established" Roman festival of December 25.

Sheffield's Professor Hughes adds: "I've been writing widely on the subject since the 1970s and it's an immensely emotive subject both from an astronomical and theological point of view. And it also has to be said a bit of minefield for us astronomers

"We can approximate, using our wonderful latest technology to a fantastic extent – but as a veteran of this subject, I long for the finding of a conclusive piece of evidence – maybe in the form of a new scroll etc. which will pinpoint a given event.

"According to Matthew, when the Wise Men arrived in Jerusalem they asked Herod, 'Where is he who is born King of the Jews? For we have seen his star in the east and have come to worship him'.

"Herod had no idea what they were talking about and had to summon his own advisers who, recalling Micah Chapter 5 Verse 2, prophesied a Messiah would be born in Bethlehem. It perhaps goes beyond the realms of astronomy, but we perhaps also have to be mindful that the Star may have been the object of useful Biblical spin – and perhaps wonder if it ever existed at all. Whatever the truth, as is evidently the case, it truly was a star of wonder."

STAR STORIES

Planets can appear to "stop" in the sky relative to the earth's orbit just as a speeding car on a motorway can appear to "go backwards" relative to another. It's called retrograde motion.

Much of the account of the appearance of the Star appears in the Gospel of St Matthew

The brilliant conjunction of Venus/Jupiter on June 17 2BC is well known in astronomy and can be viewed with any good astro software.

Experts think that the wise men were actually priests from Persia who rode to the Holy Land on horseback. Rather than kings, the Magi were priests of Zoroastrianism, the main religion of the Persian Empire.

The closest approach of Halley's Comet to the period was in approx 12BC.

10 SHEDDING NEW LIGHT ON ILKLEY MOOR

THE word 'Swastika' and imagery of such still sends a shiver down the spine these days for obvious reasons.

But high above Ilkley, at the edge of the famous moor, lie the crude, some say Neolithic markings of the mysterious 'Swastika Stone', a remnant from the ancient past, and a time when the term 'swastika' had quite the opposite connotations to its modern day implications.

For more than 3,000 years, the word swastika – taken from the Sanskrit 'su-asti-ka' meaning 'to be good' or 'to be well' - has had benign historical meanings, not just throughout numerous pagan creation myths from the past, but also in those beliefs beyond Judaism, Christianity and Islam.

Only since the 1930s onwards with the rise of Nazi Germany, has the symbol become the antithesis, ironically, of everything the original symbol was deemed to reflect, for reasons best left to historians.

Ilkley's 'Swastika Stone' – deemed important enough to be guarded by railings just on the edge of Ilkley Moor –unique in style Britain and one of only a few similar designs throughout the world – has been in situ for possibly as many as 4,000 years and has been the subject of myth, counter myth and rumour for at least the last 100 years.

The' cup and ring' rock engraving (pictured) is at best a vague swastika shape – in fact, to the casual passer-by, it would hardly merit the name; but comparisons with the 'old' swastikas of Hindu origin, and those which are scattered richly throughout world history, are striking.

The markings show an alignment of nine 'cups' or ball-bearing sized bore holes in the rocks on Woodhouse Crag, interwoven with an enclosed snaking ring shape which itself forms a rudimentary swastika shape. A tenth cup, partly encircled, lies to the side of the arrangement.

Each of the Stone's arms point to compass points; due north – within one degree - towards Simon's Seat, close to Bolton Abbey; east, towards Almscliff Crag, while the tenth rogue cup, also easterly, has long been thought to point to the position of the sun at the dawning of the summer solstice.

Some scholars believe the markings have a Celtic connection with St Brigid, and that Brigantia, the goddess worshiped by the Brigantes tribe of Northern England, (meaning 'after Brigid' or 'the people of Brigid') is synonymous with her name.

Devotees of St Brigid's - with strong associations in Ireland – would often make a cross from straw; the design of these varied from place to place but often resembled a swastika or 'sun wheel'. It's perhaps significant that the Brigantes were active around Ilkley.

As Britain's invading Romans marched northwards from 79 AD onwards, they abutted the Celtic Brigantes tribe - one time allies, and then later overran them and the Pennines to establish hill a fort in Ilkley, near All Saints Church, and outposts at Adel, among others.

All Saints Church/Manor House complex exhibited within its grounds an altar stone to the water goddess Verbeia, which also corresponds to the name of the 'goddess of Wharfedale', apparently the figure of a woman holding two serpents or either being flanked by two rivers.

The stone bears the words in Latin: 'To holy Verbeia, [made by] Clodius Fronto, prefect of the Second Cohort of Lingones.'

The Ilkley regiment contained 500 foot soldiers who were originally recruited from among the Celtic-turned-Roman Lingones tribe inhabiting the Adriatic coast of Northern Italy, the old province of Cisalpine Gaul, but one-time migrants from the Lingones region of Eastern France, close to the Champagne region, flanked by the rivers Marne and Seine.

Could the Ilkley stone have been carved by a Celtic-influenced, Verbeia/Brigid-equivalent-worshipping second century AD Roman cohort, or even by Ilkley's subdued Brigantes remembering the sun wheels of their Celtic past?

The evidence is perhaps circumstantial at best, but the fact that the 'Swastika Stone' is almost identical in form to a design called the 'Celtic' Cammunian Rose (see pic), found in rocks overlooking the river valleys of northern Italy in Val Cominica is perhaps more than coincidental. The Italian markings depict a hunter to the left of the design.

In 2004, claims were made that markings were found in Brisbane, Australia were identical to those of the 'Stone' above Ilkley Moor and even a suggestion that the markings represented the very first boomerang.

Perhaps as an even more remote chance, the solution might lie in new technology and the heavens. Polaris is well known as the Pole Star today, but due to the wobble or 'precession' of the imperfect sphere of the earth, well known to astronomers, it has not always been so.

Before Polaris, the last significant star to be at the north celestial pole – the point around which the heavens appear to revolve – was the star Thuban – in around 2750 BC, at the time of the early Bronze Age in Britain. Anyone with readily-available basic desktop astronomy software can easily determine this.

The major constellation rotating around Thuban was Draco – the Dragon or Serpent, and to a lesser degree Ursa Minor, contained within the arms of the 'dragon'.

Again it may be pure coincidence, but Draco bisects Thuban, and could be viewed as exhibiting 'bent arms' around Thuban's rotating point at this period on Earth at the four major points of the year.

Perhaps significantly, Hercules, the warrior constellation, is immediately 'next door' at this distant time – a mirror, perhaps, of Italy's Cammunian Rose? At this point the line between fact and supposition becomes increasingly blurred, but certainly a Bronze Age inhabitant of Ilkley Moor would have seen the stars swirling around Thuban and not Polaris.

His Egyptian contemporaries would, it seems, have certainly been aware of this, and recent evidence suggests what were once thought to be angular 'air shafts' in the Great Pyramid were actually astronomical devices or windows pointing towards Thuban, the then Pole.
What is known is that in Britain, the common name given to the swastika by Anglo Saxons was Fylfot, said to have been derived from the Anglo-Saxon fower fot, meaning four-footed, or many-footed.

Several well-intentioned world movements currently exist aiming to restore the swastika icon -still banned in Germany - to its pre-Nazi connotations. Whatever the outcome of the debate, it's unlikely the icon, for good or bad, will disappear, from the moor or in human culture, for some time yet.

11 TURKEY, TRIMMINGS AND 22 CTS

GOLD has long been worshipped by the ancients – notably kings at this festive season – but this year, the joy of the gilded turkey will, it seems, be gracing certain Christmas dinner tables.

Whether the height of Christmas chic, or a shining metaphor for all that is of questionable taste, golden-coated turkeys – literally the nation's favourite Christmas fowl sporting a full coat of gold leaf - look set to be the latest culinary craze.

Not as alarming as it sounds, gold is edible and largely harmless and is a popular inclusion in drinks in Britain and on the continent, albeit in small flakes.

Chefs with a flair for a particular kind of festive alchemy are already drooling at the prospect of cooking up the sort of bird Auric Goldfinger might welcome to the Christmas table.

And BBC Food blogger and writer Stefan Gates says for those with a taste for flair, the bling is the thing this Christmas.

He says: "The gold costs about the same as a bottle of cheap Champagne. So, yes, it's not cheap, but I think it's a small price to pay for a Christmas lunch that you'll never forget.

"Gold is perfectly safe to eat: its food additive E175 for anyone who was watching my last TV series! It passes straight through you and doesn't taste of anything - other than pure magic.

"For maximum effect it's best to do this secretly and only reveal what you've done when the turkey hits the table.

"It takes about 15 minutes to gild using a combination of loose leaf and transfer leaf, although I have used gold leaf a fair bit, so it may take longer.

"You need a booklet of gold at least 23ct or above, and you can get it cheaply from retail or online art shops - or expensively from edible gold leaf suppliers.

"It usually comes in booklets of 25 x 80x80mm leaves in either loose leaf (which works best) or transfer leaf (where the leaf sits on a piece of paper).

"One booklet is just enough to do a 4kg/8lb 11oz bird if you manage to do it without too much wastage. Keep any spare gold for knocking up golden sausages and mash another time."

"If you've got loose gold leaf (that's the best sort), the technique I've developed is to hold the booklet firmly so that the gold leaves don't all slip out (it's so thin that it floats away very easily, even on your own breath), then open each page gently and press the gold from the booklet straight onto the bird. Use a dry brush to dab it into place if you need to, around legs and crevices. It takes a couple of goes to get right, but then it's dead easy. Just keep going until you've covered the whole bird.

"Transfer gold leaf is great, but can give a slightly patchy effect, rather than the appearance of pure golden turkey. The transfer leaf is the easiest to use – you just need to press it against the slightly fatty skin and the gold should come away from the paper. It may need a little help with the back of a fingernail to help it, and if your gold is particularly sticky, you may need to dampen the skin of the turkey with an extra little bit of oil or a very light smear of butter. Once you've gilded the turkey as best you can, serve it with your favourite veg."

Gold leaf, flake or dust is used on and in some gourmet foods, notably sweets and drinks as decorative ingredient.

Gold flake was used by the nobility in Medieval Europe as a decoration in food and drinks, in the form of leaf, flakes or dust, either to demonstrate the host's wealth or in the belief that something that valuable and rare must be beneficial for one's health. Gold foil along with silver is sometimes used in South Asian sweets such as barrio.

Danger Goldwasser is a traditional German herbal liqueur produced in what is today Gdańsk, Poland, and Schwabach, Germany, and contains flakes of gold leaf.

There are also some expensive $100 cocktails which contain flakes of gold leaf.

However, since metallic gold is inert to all body chemistry, it adds no taste nor has it any other nutritional effect and leaves the body unaltered.

Chef and Yorkshireman Brian Turner, originally from Halifax, speaking from London, said:

"I can see the attraction of the gold but personally I think it is a bit daft. I'd much rather either have a bottle of champagne or advise people to put the equivalent amount of money in a charity box for their favourite cause in these hard times. Yorkshire folk are famous for being careful with their money and I think they'll see sense when it comes to cooking for the Xmas table as always."

Mr Turner is a honorary doctorate from both Sheffield Hallam University and Leeds Met University and a culinary legend.

Three-times Michelin-starred chef Marco Pierre White, who was born in Leeds, says:

"If people want to put gold leaf on their turkeys then good luck to them. People have been using gold in cooking for years, especially in chocolate, to great effect.

"But the best dish is still traditional turkey on Christmas Day. I will be enjoying Honey Roast Ham on Boxing Day, traditional turkey on Christmas Day and then a lovely roast goose on New Year's Day. The most important thing is that people enjoy themselves whatever they do over the season. We should also raise a glass to the great Bernard Matthews who played such an important role in making turkey – which was once expensive – so affordable to everyone. Happy Christmas everybody."

◦Stefan's blog and further details on how to create a gilded turkey can be found at the highly popular BBC Food website at: http://www.bbc.co.uk/blogs/food/2010/11/stefan-gates-golden-turkey.shtml

12 RIGHT ON TRACK FOR ART SUCCESS

A PASSION for the wonders of Yorkshire's scenery, combined with a new career as a train driver, has set a former engineer on track as an acclaimed artist.

Silsden's Martin Williamson, 48, re-kindled a passion for art after putting his life back on the rails when he swapped engineering for train driving.

Martin returned to university in the late 1980s after finding his engineering career in Crosshills was coming to a halt and then spent over a decade in the hectic world of public relations, animation, graphics, and marketing.

But it was after a second career change that he took up train driving across Yorkshire and beyond - and found the exhilaration unexpectedly re-ignited his passion for art.

Martin's striking expressionist paintings of Yorkshire and further afield have since attracted a strong online interest, as well as sales across the UK, in the United States and in Europe.

And he reckons he is in the best possible position at the front of the train to get inspiration for his next work of art.

He says:

"I started out life as an engineer and after ten years realised I was in completely the wrong job. My wife and I decided to take a very big plunge and I went back to college. At that point I was married with a mortgage and we basically survived on baked beans and fresh air for about five years – it was tough.

"I graduated in 1991 with a degree in graphic design, animation and illustration, straight into the last recession. I was all set to join an animation house in Manchester, but a franchise was lost and things didn't materialise as I thought they would. So I ended up freelancing for 18 months trying to find all sorts of bits and pieces to do to scrape a living.

"One such project was doing cartoon illustrations for the Dalesman, which I did for a number of years. In that period I also created a cartoon-illustrated calendar for two years for the local paper in Skipton – the Craven Herald.

"I then developed strong links with the media after moving into public relations for many years for a national charity and then later moved into marketing for Craven College in Skipton.

"The train driving came about when a nasty virus forced me off work for a few months and I started to think again about my future direction. My wife brought home the Yorkshire Post one day which was running an advertisement for train drivers.

"It was something I had never thought of; I have always had an interest in railways without actually standing on the platforms and collecting numbers.

"When I left school in the seventies, the railways were struggling and I never considered train-driving as a career option. But 30 years on it's a thriving industry, I applied – along with about two thousand other hopefuls – for a place in the training school at York and the rest is history. That was seven years ago and that's what I now do full time.

"The great thing about working shifts is I get quite a few days off in the week, and that's where the painting fits in.
"It also takes me across the county as well – the longest run I currently do is via Lancaster to Morecambe; I tend to carry a notebook or small sketchbook with me to make a note of ideas when I get a break away from the cab.

"Certainly, driving over Ribblehead Viaduct just as the sun is rising is an artist's dream and begs to be painted - I'm in the best seat on the train to see it.

"I'm based in Skipton so I normally do the Leeds-Bradford-Ilkley commuter routes, but we also do a morning and an evening run to Ribblehead as well as the Morecambe and Lancaster services.

"I've been painting now for about two years. It all started as a result of going away with Barbara to the Isle of Mull for our silver wedding anniversary. Being surrounded by all that fantastic scenery and seeing local artist's work displayed in the island's galleries, I thought 'I bet I could do that.'

"I had always drawn, but I had never really painted, and it really kicked off from there - people seemed to like what I do.

"I exhibited locally last year at an open exhibition in Keighley but most of my work is exhibited and sold through an online presence. I set up my own website and created a Facebook page about a year ago; hundreds of people from all around the globe have now joined my page."

Martin's artwork covers landscapes, ancient buildings and churches across the UK, and has featured local landmarks such as Ilkley Moor, Bolton Abbey, East Riddlesden Hall, Skipton Castle, Haworth and Gawthorpe Hall just over the border in Lancashire. He uses a variety of media such as inks, oil pastels and acrylics in a highly individual and bold Impressionist, expressive style.

"I don't actively sell them, for me the satisfaction is in the creation – if people like my work it is a bonus; but I've sold paintings to people in America and Europe and throughout the UK.

"It's all rapid stuff – I like to do a painting in around 20 to 30mins, so I try not to get bogged down with detail at all, leaving the viewer's imagination to fill the gaps for themselves.

"I'm delighted to be combining a new career with a revitalised skill – we are lucky to have such wonderful landscape and buildings in this county - and I hope the good people of Yorkshire appreciate the passion - and the stimulus - behind my art."

• Martin's striking site and works can be found at www.cobbybrook.co.uk and www.facebook/cobbybrook

13 THE LOST BOW

LOVERS of picturesque Wharfedale are being urged to help solve a mystery surrounding the unearthing of an old longbow in a disused chapel in the heart of the Dales.

The ancient bow, initially thought to be an English longbow, has been discovered near Bolton Abbey in beautiful Wharfedale.

The discovery was made beneath floorboards in the unused chapel of The Priests House, part of the Grade I listed Barden Tower complex, near Barden Bridge, Burnsall, N Yorkshire.

It was built and occupied by Henry Clifford , Yorkshire's "The Shepherd Lord" of legend.

Now a well-known restaurant with medieval banqueting facilities, run by Leeds restaurateur Debbie Leathley and husband Steve, the Priests House is the extant and thriving part of the ruin of Barden Tower, which dates back to at least the 16th Century.

The six-foot tall bow – which is in remarkable condition, but minus the drawstring - was found by head chef Mark Finch beneath floorboards of the old, deconsecrated and disused chapel, which lies beneath the restaurant.

Attempts to solve the mystery of the bow have so far involved actor Robert Hardy – Siegfried Farnon in BBC TV's All Creatures Great and Small - a respected authority on the history of the longbow, among others.

However scientific testing by the Royal Armouries in Leeds have turned initial assumptions on their head, creating an even more puzzling picture for the historical detectives just when they thought they were on target with their assumptions.

The bow has been identified as a bamboo bow from the Chota Nagpur region of Central India, a type which was commonly used by the hill tribes in days gone by.

Steve says:

"Exactly how this ended up in rural Yorkshire hidden away for perhaps hundreds of years is a complete mystery and one with which we would like so help. Is it evidence of the extent of the ancient trade routes or perhaps a gift brought back from abroad? I guess we will never know but we'd like to appeal to readers to help solve this curious mystery."

Steve and Debbie are supporting the Bolton Abbey estate, English Heritage and local planners in developing an appraisal for converting the disused chapel into a prestigious new function venue and dining space which would sit in spectacular scenery above Barden Bridge and the River Wharfe.

It was whilst tidying up the ancient disused chapel in advance of a visit that the bow was unearthed.

It was found purely by chance beneath floorboards close to the altar of the ancient chapel, which had been boarded-up, and which was being used as a storage area.

Author , businessman and medieval history consultant Peter Algar, from Horsforth, author of the highly-respected The Shepherd Lord novel, was called in by Steve and Debbie to help shed light on the find.

He says all early indications seemed to point to it being a bow of medieval origin.

"We initially thought it might belong to one of Yorkshire's best known local heroes. The legend of Henry Clifford, the so-called Shepherd Lord, is very well known in Yorkshire, especially around Skipton and the rural areas of the Dales and into Lancashire. But significantly, he has an important link with Barden Tower.

"Henry lost his aristocratic father in the War of the Roses and, as heir to his estates in Skipton and surrounding areas, fled into the wilds of Yorkshire.

"He was unsuccessfully hunted down by Edward IV as a result of some bad blood between the then ruling Yorkist faction and the local Clifford family, who lived at Skipton Castle.

"As a result, he was brought up as a shepherd boy in the wilds of Yorkshire before he was eventually restored to his estates much later under Henry VII.

"Steve and Debbie consulted me on the strength of my novel, The Shepherd Lord, which is a 'reimagining' of the legend. But what is certain is Henry Clifford's connection with Barden Tower and the Priests House – and the mysterious chapel.

Peter, from Horsforth, Leeds, who is widely respected for his knowledge of medieval Yorkshire history, says:

"Barden Tower was a traditional hunting lodge, in fact the nearby Forest of Barden was used as hunting grounds in the 15th C. Henry Clifford, after his restoration to his estates following his life lived in the wild, rebuilt it and made it his principal residence.

"He needed a place of calm so that he could re-connect with his rustic upbringing and – given he was illiterate – get an all-round education. In fact, he had the chapel built under the mezzanine of the Priests House for this purpose.

"He used the tall towers as an observatory to look at the night sky, under the expert tuition of the Prior of nearby Bolton Abbey. When he was a boy, he was fascinated by the night sky, an interest fostered by the solitude of tending his flocks on the fells.

"It is under the floorboards of the chapel, a room untouched for over a century, that the longbow was found."

Debbie Leathley, from Pudsey, Leeds, who run the Priests House restaurant with husband Steve in 2004, says:

"This building is quite fascinating, we never know what we might stumble across next. Today it is an ancient Indian bow, yesterday a ghost playing the piano, and tomorrow? Who knows? What I can say is that if the restoration of the chapel does go ahead then I am sure we will uncover something else of interest"

Peter adds:

"The bow is over six foot tall and preserved in a dark coating. It is one piece flat bow and differs from that of a traditional longbow, which has rounded limbs that are circular or D shaped in cross-section.

"It was likely used for hunting, as Barden used to have its own deer park, or perhaps for target practice as archery was very popular in past times and after ecommendation from our resident archaeologist, Tim Sutherland, it was agreed to take it for dating and expert analysis to the Royal Armouries at Leeds.

"It is hand crafted and the bowyer knew what he was doing as he left the knots in when shaving the bow staff to maintain its strength. It must therefore have taken a reasonably strong draw weight.

"I consulted Robert Hardy is an acknowledged expert on the longbow and who was consulted when a large cache of bows like these were discovered in the hold of the Marie Rose, Henry VIII's flagship.

"Under the auspices of the Towton Battlefield Society, "It looks more like a hunting bow than war bow but the people I have spoken to say it is certainly significant and has got one or two people baffled. Even if not from the period, it's an important find for Yorkshire and the region."

* More info on The Priests House can be found at http://www.thepriestshouse.co.uk/

* George Peter Algar's personal history of The Shepherd Lord and associated novel can be found at www.theshepherdlord.com. Peter writes under the nom-de-plume of George Peter Algar.

14 A TOUCH OF G AND S IN THE NIGHT

LOVERS of Gilbert and Sullivan's popular comic operettas are marking the next step in the development of one of the oldest – if not THE oldest – G&S Society in the UK.

The multi-award winning Leeds Gilbert and Sullivan Society – which has already entered its second century of songs, shows and sophisticated silliness – has grown exponentially since humble beginnings in the terraced streets of the city.

Organisers and enthusiasts from the 150-strong society now hope to introduce a new generation to the musical satires, stage delights and clever social observations of the staged works of Messrs W S Gilbert and Arthur Sullivan.

The society – which has a regular rehearsal and performance base at the Carriageworks Theatre off Millennium Square, Leeds – staged the Yeomen of the Guard this year (March 2011), and is already actively preparing and recruiting for its next major performance of the topically satirical Iolanthe in March 2012.

Publicity secretary and cast member Katie Lister says although Leeds-based, the society boasts members from across Yorkshire and beyond and has enthusiasts aged 13-70 years old plus.

And while the troupe is looking to its future - with exciting plans to expand further its touring base and membership from across Yorkshire , Ms Lister says the society's illustrious history and the infectious appeal of the genius of the Victorian duo, remain key to its success.

She says the pair's innate ability to adroitly reflect the absurdity of social situation remains both timeless and universal.

"Their works are as popular as ever – and just as relevant in the 21st C as Iolanthe demonstrates. Their plots are topsy-turvy, but very funny and charming at the same time – and often have some moments of real pathos in them.

"Sullivan's music can range from stirring marches via rousing choruses, to pretty ballets and lovely duets. He was incredibly talented and his music fits the plots perfectly. I still get goose bumps with certain numbers, even though I know them inside out.

"Iolanthe, which we're performing in March 2012, is a great example of their satirical mastery; among other things, it pokes fun at the starchy House of Lords and politicians, so is still topical.

"G&S are part of our heritage; whole generations were brought up on them, from church societies to schools, a lot of people have cut their musical teeth on their music. And a lot of professional opera companies perform them nowadays, where historically they might have sneered at such. Opera North performed Ruddigore last year, for example.

"In Victorian times, there was nothing else like them in their day, and they were accessible and relevant to a huge cross-section of the population and caught their imagination – very much like the Tim Rice and Andrew Lloyd Webber of their time. That's why they continue to be popular – and still have that magic touch."

The two men collaborated on fourteen comic operas between 1871 and 1896, of which HMS Pinafore, the Pirates of Penzance and The Mikado are among the best known.

Gilbert was born in London on 18 November 1836. His father was a naval surgeon who later wrote novels and short stories, some of which included illustrations by his son.

In 1861, to supplement his income, the younger Gilbert began writing illustrated stories, poems and articles of his own, many of which would later be used as inspiration for his plays and operas, particularly Gilbert's series of illustrated poems.

Sullivan was born in London on 13 May 1842. His father was a military bandmaster, and by the time Arthur had reached the age of eight, he was proficient with all the instruments in the band.

But it was the theatre manager and impresario Richard D'Oyly-Carte who commissioned the pair when searching for a new form of English light opera which would replace the bawdy burlesques of London at the time.

He assembled a syndicate and formed the Comedy Opera Company, with Gilbert and Sullivan commissioned to write a comic opera that would serve as the centrepiece for an evening's entertainment.

The Sorcerer opened in London in 1877 to success and critical acclaim, but it was HMS Pinafore, in 1878 which propelled the pair to international fame.

During the run of Pinafore, Richard D'Oyly Carte split up with his former investors. The disgruntled former partners, who had each invested in the production with no return, staged a public fracas, sending a group of thugs to seize the scenery during one performance.

Stagehands successfully managed to ward off their backstage attackers but this event cleared the way for Carte, Gilbert and Sullivan to form the D'Oyly Carte Opera Company, which then produced all of their succeeding operas.

H.M.S. Pinafore ran in London for 571 performances, the second longest run of any musical theatre piece in history up to that time.

And a little like the subjects of the operettas, a broad range of people from all walks of Leeds life have graced the society's stages.

Katie says:

"The Society was formed in Hunslet in Leeds. Among all the heavy industry of the area lived a large community of people, mainly living in hundreds of terraced houses, now long-since demolished, which had been built to accommodate factory workers, hence the name "South Accommodation Road".

"The Vicar of St Silas'Methodist Church, The Rev S Froggatt, (the President of the first Society) was concerned about pollution for the inhabitants of the area and had commented that '..from the vicarage windows we can see about 40 chimneys'.

"It was against this background that the "Hunslet St Silas Choral and Operatic Society" was formed by a group of young people 'as a means of healthy recreation and to foster and develop a love of music in Hunslet.' "

"Members originally had to be Churchgoers and to live within the tiny St Silas parish boundaries.

"In the 1930s, the Society decided to invite members of the other three parishes in Hunslet to join their ranks and after WW II, with a bank balance of £25.0s.7d, and a membership of 34, the Society became known as the Hunslet Choral & Operatic Society.

"Performances of choral works such as "The Holy City", "Olivet to Calvary" were given in church and musicals, which included "The Mandarin", "Princess JuJu" and "The Bandolero, " as well as Gilbert and Sullivan operettas, were presented annually at St Joseph's Hall, Hunslet.

"Rehearsals took place in the St Silas Church schoolroom on Monday evenings (which is still our rehearsal night) until 1953.

"When St Silas was scheduled for demolition, the rehearsal venue was moved to the factory canteen of TF & JH Braime Pressings on Hunslet Road when Ronald Braime became the Society's President.

"At the same time, the name was changed to "The Leeds Gilbert and Sullivan Society" and for 52 years, annual performances of G&S took place at Leeds Civic Theatre.

"Now, with a slightly larger bank balance, and with over 150 members and Friends, rehearsals and annual performances now take place at The Carriageworks off Millennium Square.

"It goes without saying that we are deeply indebted to those visionary young people who started such a small society so many years ago and, already into our next century, we are looking towards the next chapter in our history with optimistic enthusiasm.

"Some tread the boards and others work backstage, as crew, makeup, costumes, front of house and in the production team and whole families are encouraged to take part.

"We welcome new members in any capacity so if anyone fancies themselves being in the chorus or prefers to be based backstage, we'd love to hear from them for either a chat or a not-too-daunting audition!"

Rehearsals are already scheduled for Iolanthe in 2012 and more can be found at the contact details below.

Full details can be found at the Leeds G&S Society's web site at: www.leedsgands.org.uk.or email: committee@leedsgands.org.uk

- Iolanthe was the first of Gilbert and Sullivan's operas to premiere at the Savoy. The story concerns a band of immortal fairies who find themselves at odds with the House of Lords. The opera satirises many aspects of British government and law.

- The Society has also performed/rehearsed in Filey Methodist Church, Chapel Allerton, Bedale, and at Leeds Grammar School and welcome members from across Yorkshire.

15 RICHARD III UNDER FIRE

Actor Kevin Spacey and renowned director Sam Mendes might be wowing the theatrical world with their 'modern dress' interpretation of Shakespeare's Richard III, but not all are impressed with the goings-on at the Old Vic.

The play unites Spacey with director Sam Mendes for the first time since the 1999 movie "American Beauty" which earned both men an Academy Award.

Set in the 15th century and depicting the bloody journey of Richard, Duke of Gloucester and the path he takes to become Richard III, the new interpretation has been one of the most highly anticipated in the British theatre.

However Mendes' recent newspaper and online remarks comparing Richard III to today's modern dictators, have raised the hackles of at least one group which fights to defend the name of arguably Britain's most maligned monarch.

Mendes was reported as saying in recent major press (via the Reuters Press Agency and others) that he was inspired by parallels between Richard III and the contemporary political upheaval in North Africa.

He is reported to have said: "'We are living in an era in which figures such as Richard, i.e. (Libyan leader Muammar) Gaddafi, (former Egyptian President Hosni) Mubarak etc., are on the front page of every newspaper again," he said.

"What Shakespeare wrote about seems remarkably similar to what is happening in front of our eyes. It felt like the perfect time to do that.'"

But the comparison has brought anger from the respected Richard III Foundation Inc. which claims the remarks are in bad taste.

CEO Joe-Ann Ricca, in an open letter from the organisation, published on the society's website in the early of this morning, says:

"'For centuries, Shakespeare's Richard III has enthralled audiences, the sixteenth century's pre-eminent playwright's depiction of an evil, villainous hunch-back sending ripples of fear and loathing down theatre goers spines.

'And this is probably the exact effect Shakespeare wanted. But it would seem that, when it comes to Shakespeare, not only theatre goers, but actors and directors as well, have lost sight of the fact that William Shakespeare was a dramatist, not an historian, working to curry favour with the ruling power at the time, the Tudors - the family that did everything in its power to obliterate Richard III and his lineage.

'This was made abundantly clear when Kevin Spacey, artistic director of the Old Vic and star of the new Richard III production, and director Sam Mendes shockingly and appalling compared the deceased monarch to Moammar Gadhafi [sic] and Hosni Mubarak - men accused of, among many things, the premeditated murder of peaceful protesters; illegal hidden detention facilities; state corruption on a massive level; crimes against humanity; state sponsored terrorism and the mass raping of women. Crimes that not even Richard III's harshest critics have attempted to attribute to his short reign.

'Spacey went on to state that these modern dictators base their idea of kingship on English monarchy - a statement that should raise more than a few eyebrows, to say the least. If this is true, then God help England.'"

She adds:

"'It is true that Shakespeare's play has long been a source of contention for Ricardians working to restore the reputation of England's most controversial king. The lack of documentary evidence regarding Richard's reign was destroyed by his successor, if one can call him that, Henry VII. Henry VII left a dearth of material to draw from to corroborate facts, and separate the truth from fiction and, when it comes to Shakespeare, artistic freedom.

'Mr. Spacey is an outstanding actor with an impressive resume, both on and off the screen. His work with the Old Vic and the Bridge Project is highly commendable and deserves recognition. He and Mendes forward-thinking, creative approach to a modernized version of Shakespeare's centuries old work is admirable. And yes, this is just a play. A modern interpretation of something performed thousands of times before. A new take on the tired and worn-out myth created by Shakespeare is long overdue.

'But what would be truly unique and different would be for an actor and director to take the time to study and research history of an historic figure, combining modern knowledge and deeper character assessment for a more profound production. For Spacey and Mendes to compare someone that they obviously know nothing or very little about to the Gadhafi's and Mubaraks of the world is a discredit to their work and the production, not to mention the good name of King Richard III."'

The Richard III Foundation Inc. is a non-profit educational organization that was founded in 1994.

It is proud to state that it is the only organization that does not take a neutral view of the last Yorkist King.

Ms Ricca adds: "Continued research has been shown that the Yorkist period was one of progress and enlightened government. It is our sense of injustice to Richard III's reputation that enforces our belief that the truth is worth fighting for and one of the many reasons the Foundation was established."

A spokeswoman for the Old Vic Theatre in London declined to comment on the matter.

- The Foundation's website can be found at www.richard111.com and has close links with Middleham in N Yorkshire

- Richard was Governor of the North for a brief period and still has loyal support in the N of England today in some quarters.

- More can be found at www.oldvictheatre.com

"The world is grown so bad, that wrens make prey where eagles dare not perch." - from Richard III.

16 THOU ART FIRED

Almost four centuries after his death, William Shakespeare's famous words: "All the world's a stage and all the men and women merely players", might be more readily revised as "all the world's a business and all the men and women merely clients".

On the 400th anniversary of the writing of what was probably his last solo-penned play, The Tempest, and as the economy prepares itself for choppy waters in the wake of the greatest public sector cuts in a generation, should business leaders take their perhaps unlikely cue from the master writer?

While Shakespeare's art is unquestioned, and his power of language known throughout the world, academics are increasingly looking at his business acumen, and what gave him, in cruder 21st century terms, the X factor from a celebrity and business point of view.

Surprisingly to some, American businessmen are even citing Shakespeare and his works as the new business motivational, asking employees if they are the Hamlet of the boardroom –

disinherited and hesitant – or the Goneril or Regan of a family business, scheming and grasping.

While Will might not seem to be the obvious candidate for business models in hard times, by the time he died he left an estate worth at least £2m in today's terms, and had a substantial reputation as a gentleman and businessman.

And coming out of the age of Elizabethan exuberance into the more sober times of the court of James I, some reckon Shakespeare was perfectly placed to witness the changing economic times.

Academics say his skills as a businessman are there for all to see in black and white.

Prof David Lindley, from the University of Leeds, says that while Shakespeare's relatively- modest background and education have persuaded some to question his qualifications for writing the 38 plays, the sonnets and poems, his business mind was as sharp as his language skills.

"While everyone knows of Shakespeare the dramatist – he is, still, the only author that virtually every school pupil must read – his ability as a businessman is an aspect of his achievement which is all too often overlooked," he says. "Shakespeare was a writer, but he was also an actor, a sharer in a theatrical company and part-owner of a playhouse (the Globe, and later the Blackfriars theatres).

"Yes of course, he was a superb writer, but he was also aware of the economics of the theatre – to put it crudely the 'bums on seats' of the business, or in today's parlance the need for 'clients'.

"It's an aspect which is all too often overlooked in studies of Shakespeare – especially at high school level.

"He wasn't of 'noble' stock as such so he didn't have the advantage of old money on which to fall back. His father was a glover, and while for a time a very much respected man in Stratford, his fortunes actually seem to have declined in later years, so Shakespeare probably did not have much, if anything, behind him."

Prof Lindley says that by the late 16th century, when he was in his 30s, Shakespeare had clearly made a fair amount of money – in 1597 he was in a position to buy New Place, one of the largest and most sought-after properties in Stratford, and to make other investments in his home town in the years that followed.

"While his play writing would have made his name, he was successful financially through his position as a 'sharer' in the Globe Theatre itself, and a member of the most successful theatrical company of the day, which came to be known as The King's Men.

"As a playwright he would never really have made it to any sort of 'A' list as we know it today – such a list would be made up exclusively of premier aristocrats and courtiers, but his skills were second to none, and he certainly was noticed by a number of his contemporaries as a major figure on the literary landscape.

"In other words, he was in the right place at the right time – artistically, aesthetically, and from a business point of view."

London theatres represented a revolution in culture, being the first capitalist businesses in the world built entirely around entertainment. The heart of this cultural business model was the actors' company, in which a group of actors invested money in a common stock of properties, costumes and plays and, while old Shakespeare may have been happiest writing iambic pentameter, according to business gurus he also had a keen eye for leadership, a skill which has apparently changed little in the last 400 years.

"Shakespeare is timelessly wise and eternally popular, and his plays are packed with essential insights into human psychology and the use and abuse of power," says Norman Augustine, co-author of Shakespeare in Charge (Talk Miramax Books), a guide to Shakespeare strategies for CEOs, and former board member at Procter and Gamble, Black and Decker and others. "Like almost no other dramatist, Shakespeare looks deeply into what it takes to be a leader, and how leaders need to act under demanding and extreme circumstances.

"Whether it is looking at Henry V's amazing ability to motivate a team facing almost certain defeat and turn the situation around, or King Lear demonstrating the perils of poor estate management, the Bard reveals his management genius in its full glory."

So could the man who has for so long been at the centre of England's cultural heritage, really have lessons for today's business leaders?

"It was the ownership of theatre and company that gave Shakespeare his financial success," adds Professor Martin Butler, also from the University of Leeds. "You only have to look at the careers of other playwrights to see that writing wasn't a way to wealth. You don't find Christopher Marlowe or Ben Jonson at the centre of complex property deals. What sets Shakespeare apart is his investment in theatre as an institution.

"That said, it could be added that his company was probably a comparatively democratic business, focussing on the team rather than the individual businessman.

"There was a group of sharers (or stock-holders, as we'd say now) who all had an equal stake, and they weren't just a board of directors but workers who actively made the product from which they benefited. Hence one imagines there must always have been a lot of give and take between Shakespeare and his fellows.

"Shakespeare is interested in the psychology of leadership, that doesn't mean we have to see him as necessarily endorsing it; he registers the costs as well as the benefits. So, for example, Henry V becomes a great leader of men, but the cost is he has to turn away from Falstaff and his former friends."

So as everyone prepares to tighten their economic doublets, perhaps the isle of prosperity might still yet be reached, 400 years after the Bard foresaw the tempest.

17 NOTHING NEW UNDER THE SUN WHEN IT COMES TO POLITICAL CHANGE

ASTROLOGY has long been viewed by many as being the quack cousin of the 'proper' science of astronomy, but when it comes to political change and the stars, to the poetic imagination at least, it seems there really is nothing new under the sun.

Since Shakespeare's day, to writers and some stargazers, the heavens have long been the abode of portents and omens and harbingers of political upheaval.

Viewers in Yorkshire will be able to wake up to the curious heavenly conjunction of the planet Venus – the brightest of the planets - nestled just alongside the new, waxing or renewing crescent moon on Sunday May 16.

Both bodies will be close enough to appear to almost 'kiss' in the sky of the early morning - and to observers in the southern hemisphere, the most brilliant of planets will appear from behind the returning moon.

Those who read portents into such signs will no doubt make much of such, but perhaps not for the first time in history, are the stars proving to be prophetic when it comes to political machinations of earth?

Modern science has little if no truck with such 'coincidences', but history, literature and poetry are littered with celestial omens and portents reflecting or predicting changes for kings and those in power.

The planet Jupiter - which some online twitters and pseud 'sooths' have, perhaps conveniently, been observing 'shadowing' the waning crescent moon since the election on May 6 - has long been associated in lore as being the ruler of the heavens, with a direct link to mankind's machinations.

And while strictly pooh-poohed by astronomers, new moons and conjunctions of major bodies and other curious astro happenings have always presaged change and union in mythology.

Halley's Comet appearance in 1066 is well known, presaging the downfall and rise respectively of Harold and the rise of William the Conqueror.

The Roman leader Constantine the Great, according to legend, famously saw a vision in which either a cross or a fish was emblazoned above the sun in the sky.

A loud, steady voice then allegedly told him, In hoc signo vinces ("In this sign you will win"). He used the sign as a standard in battle successfully bringing Christianity to the Empire.

The later Elizabethans were even more fearful of the heavens, believing a direct relationship existed between the movement of the 'celestial orbs' and the affairs of men.

Shakespeare's Julius Caesar is packed with celestial omens and portents presaging his downfall as are King Lear and Hamlet.

At the time of Julius Caesar's first performance, Elizabeth I, was elderly and had refused to name a successor, leading to worries that a political strife similar to that of Rome might break out after her death.

But perhaps the most resonant story from history is that of Edward IV, the leader of the Yorkist faction in the deadlock of the War of the Roses.

Locked in the bitter power deadlock of 1461, he witnessed the unusual sight of three 'sundogs' – or two false suns and the genuine sun – rising in the low dawn before the decisive battle of Mortimer's Cross.

Shakespeare's play Henry VI Pt 3 – has it that his witnessing of the event – known to astronomers as 'parhelion' - spurred him on to a decisive victory which would change the course of history.

In Act Two Scene One of Henry VI Pt 3, Edward (then the Earl of March) and his political ally and 'Kingmaker' Richard Neville, Earl of Warwick exclaim:

"Dazzle my eyes or do I see three suns?

"Three glorious suns, each one a perfect sun;

Not separated with the racking clouds,

But sever'd in a pale clear-shining sky.

See, see! they join, embrace, and seem to kiss,

As if they vow'd some league inviolable:

Now are they but one lamp, one light, one sun.

In this the heaven figures some event."

Historians and writers surmise Edward and his Yorkist troops took the 'triple sun' as a portent of good luck - a 'Trinity' in highly religious times and also as an emblem.

It was not until later that they adopted the famous white rose, hence Richard's III's reference to the glorious sun of York at the start of the eponymous play.

History also, perhaps portently, recounts how Warwick, Edward's 'Kingmaker', - the wealthiest and most powerful lord of his age - later turncoated and sided with the Lancastrians to propel them to power.

Edward had ruled with Warwick's support but the pair was unable to agree on policy.

Warwick jumped ship and helped to restore Henry VI, only to be crushed in battle by his own machinations, and his original master, and the course of history changed forever.

Whatever the outcome of the current political strife, perhaps there is nothing new under the sun? Old Bill Shakespeare, where are you when we need you?

18 THE NEW KID ON THE COMPUTER BLOCK

IF the Nineties were the decade of 'dumbing down', the 2000s might well be remembered as the knowledgeable 'Noughties'.

And on the internet at least this year, the battle for our collective minds is about to joined in a clash of the cerebral cyber Titans.

Wikipedia, that online heaven and hell of journalists and door-to-door encyclopaedia salesman alike, has long been the 'quick fix' for knowledge junkies worldwide for more than ten years.

As the ultimate exponent of so-called Web 2.0 technology – or the 'do-it-yourself' web philosophy, kitchen-sink Socrates have been able to wax lyrical alongside university PhDs in an amalgam of cosmopolitan pseudo-cleverness since 2001.

And it has worked. To date, the site – constantly one of the top 10 most visited sites in the world alongside it interactive cousins MySpace and YouTube – is heading for its 3,500,000th English language entry, and the collective colossus has even begun to break news ahead of some of its rival mainstream news channels.

However, all that could be about to change. Ironically, Wikipedia's strength in its plebeian all-inclusiveness may well turn out to be its Achilles Heel, according to its erstwhile co-founder, Larry Sanger, who in 2007 launched the young pretender to the cyber crown of knowledge, the equally grandiose-sounding 'Citizendium'.

Mr Sanger, 42, honorary founding editor-in-chief, reckons his infant online encyclopaedia - still open to the masses but with a robust 'peer review' model, will, over time, ignite the imaginations of the armchair intelligentsia globally.

Sanger, alongside Jimmy Wales, the co-founder of Wikipedia, and a graduate from Ohio University and a PhD himself, hopes the perceived meritocracy of the venture - which already has the over 15,000 entries -will give it even greater mass appeal.

He says:

"In the case of Citizendium we're simply in the business of attempting to create the world's most accurate and trusted source of knowledge.

"In my view, Wikipedia has been badly governed, and is not nearly as reliable or as credible as it could be. In short, and with all due respect to so many fine Wikipedians, I think humanity can do better.

"The Citizendium began life by uploading a copy of all Wikipedia articles, and our intention was to get to work on improving and then approving Wikipedia's articles. Then, in January of 2007, we decided to delete all of the Wikipedia articles that we hadn't changed, which was the vast majority of them. Most of us felt that we would have a livelier, more productive, and better project if we started over from scratch. I think we were right.

"The project has no official or unofficial connection whatsoever with Wikipedia. I broke with Wikipedia permanently around January 2003, over the very issues (of community governance and a role for experts) that I have been raising ever since.

"We differ from Wikipedia in three main respects: we require the use of real names; we have a modest role for experts; and we are committed to professionalism and the rule of law, not to anarchism and the rule of aggressive, anonymous people.

"I think our model is better, and in the long run, the better model will be more attractive to more people, both contributors and readers."

"We are certainly not elitist; we are egalitarian as well. We are open to the general public, and it is indeed easier to become an author in our system than an expert editor, and we have ten times as many authors registered as editors.

"We merely have the sane idea that making a modest, "bottom-up" role for experts in our system will improve the outcome. So far, I think this prediction has been borne out."

Contrary to some beliefs, Mr Sanger did not become an especially rich man as result of founding Wikipedia, which, like Citizendium, has a 'not-for-profit' status officially, and a benign, intellectually philanthropic outlook.

"I think that community projects like Wikipedia and the Citizendium should be controlled, and therefore owned, by the contributors. I suppose that, like many college professors, my career path is civic minded. If I never get very rich, I will not be too disappointed. That's not what it's all about."

But will Citizendium eventually outseat its ancestral cousin in online popularity? Mr Sanger is philosophical.

"It will also take at least a few more years before we have an amount of content even close to the amount Wikipedia has now. But we can certainly be extremely useful even if we never overtake Wikipedia. Indeed, on the topics of our well-developed articles, we do pretty well already."

While some might see Mr Sanger as being a modern day pseudo-Prometheus – effectively stealing the fire from the Gods of his own creation to give to a knowledge-hungry mankind – his view of himself is engagingly humble.

"There is no doubt that Wikipedia is extremely useful, and the Citizendium project and its accelerating growth is very exciting to me. So I would be lying if I did not say I felt a little proud of my work on these projects. But only a little.

"But I wonder if, in ten years, the Citizendium might have serious drawbacks of its own? What if it becomes even more influential than Wikipedia? Then, how it is governed becomes incredibly important, and if it is poorly governed, the world could suffer as a result. I know I have been playing with fire, and this makes me nervous. Whether I ought to feel proud of these projects is something I suspect I won't be able to determine until I am an old man."

Mr Sanger is Editor-in-Chief of Citizendium, which by its own words aims to create the 'world's most trusted online encyclopaedia and knowledge base'. It can be found at www.citizendium.org.

* As of 2010, Mr Sanger holds an honorary position with relation to the project but still maintains links with Citizendium.

19 TAKEN AT THE FLOOD

It was a flood of near 'Biblical' proportions.

The 'once-in-a-lifetime' deluge which last year devastated homes and businesses in the Lake District was only supposed to happen every thousand years.

But this year, as the anniversary of the record cataclysm looms, it's perhaps understandable why hundreds of Lakeland residents are looking to the skies this November.

Images of broken bridges, flooded streets and the tragic death of a police officer hit the headlines nationally and persuaded many tourists that The Lakes was a no-go area in 2009.

As Windermere and other lakes rose by as much as three metres in the space of 48 hrs., bookings were cancelled, as far ahead as spring 2010, while the tourist board's emergency hotline received calls from people asking simply, "Can we still come to Cumbria"?

The River Derwent and the River Cocker which drain the Borrowdale and Buttermere valleys could not contain the amount of water which hit the hills.

By early afternoon on 19 Nov 2009, the main street of Cockermouth was a raging torrent. Many had to be rescued by boat from the upper floors or even the roofs of their houses.

The River Greta in Keswick also burst its banks, flooding homes and businesses.

Across Cumbria numerous bridges collapsed under the force of the water.

Around 1300 homes and businesses were destroyed by the floods in Cockermouth, Keswick, Ulverston, Workington, Kendal and other smaller communities.

In popular Bowness, the lower reaches of the town became almost indistinguishable from the advancing Lake Windermere.

Dozens of businesses moved upstairs if they could, but many succumbed to the rising tide.

And while Cumbria Tourism was quick to reassure tourists that many areas of Cumbria were unaffected, the flood impacted severely on the local economy and particularly on tourism.

The Swan Hotel & Spa in Newby Bridge recently re-opened its doors to the public following a £4million refurbishment. The popular hotel, which abuts the river front at Newby

Bridge, had its ground floor flooded in the deluge, and has undergone a major revamp, complete with a new look behind its classic façade.

According to the Met Office, the unprecedented level of rainfall was due to an Atlantic weather front becoming almost stationary over Northern Ireland, Cumbria and south-west Scotland.

The front and the south-westerly winds associated with it drew very warm, moist air up from the Azores region. The rain was intensified by the effect of the mountains causing record breaking rainfall totals. The ground was already saturated from weeks of heavy rainfall and disaster was inevitable.

The floods were indiscriminate in who and what they affected.

The Lakeside Hotel, situated on the shore of Windermere by Newby Bridge, had all of its ground floor flooded. Owners have since invested £200,000 to enhance the facilities - including its kitchens, bar, restaurant and conservatory.

And at the luxury Windermere Marina Village, in Bowness, some 20 boats sank, as staff were taken completely by surprise by the rising waters.

In fact, millions of pounds have been invested in a revamp of facilities by tourism businesses blighted by last year's floods across the area.

Many are now hoping that – in what would be a cruel twist of fate - lightning will not strike twice.

Thomas G Noblett, managing director of the prestigious Langdale Chase Hotel, which overlooks the northern shores of Windermere, says he is not the only one concerned that the flood could happen two years in a row.

He says:

"I think very many people in the Lakes will be very very nervous this November. Even as I speak, similar patterns to last year seem to be developing – we've had five days of heavy rain already and very many of the hotspots on the roads are becoming impassable with flooding.

"I reckon we lost around £25,000 in trade last year with direct loss of trade at the time and later cancellations through the misconception that Cumbria was shut, thanks a misunderstanding about a key bridge being down.

"The key factor last year was that the ground was already waterlogged when the deluge hit, which was the major influence on the rapid rise of the lake and the flooding of the valleys.

"The same cycle of weather patterns seems to be happening now and I can tell you I am very nervous for what might happen in late November again. People say it can never happen again, but I certainly wouldn't rule it out again this year.

"We are quite fortunate in that the hotel is positioned quite high above the lake, but our lower grounds were flooded and one of our expensive boats went through the roof of our boathouse when the lake rose. Of course the message to people is please come to the Lakes, but it is certainly true that many of us are looking to the skies again.

"I train daily in the lake as a keen swimmer and know the lake like the back of my hand and I have a strange feeling again about it again this year."

Jason Dearden, managing director of the Windermere Marina Village, which abuts the lake, is more cautious.

He says:

"Yes, of course everyone is nervous this November, but it is important to bear in mind that we had a series of extraordinary circumstances which led to the events of last year, most of which were probably traceable back to 2008.

"In the October of that year, we had very heavy rain followed by an unusually wet summer, and then we had a mini flood before the very heavy flood of 2009. The ground was already sodden before the extraordinary foot and a half of water which occurred in that short space of 36 hours or so in Nov 2009 hit.

"So what was very unusual in the run up to the flood was we had an 'A-B-C series' of irregular events occurring which preceded the downpour.

"Although it is has been raining heavily so far in November this year, we have had the driest period from Jan-Jun this year in 74 years – at some stages near drought conditions - so I think if the rain were to happen again, that there would be some take up capacity in the ground and in the Langdales.

There's also a lot more awareness in Bowness and in the region generally.

"We have invested some £3.5m since the flood at the village and the marina and have been working very closely with the Environment Agency which is undertaking a lake level study on an on-going basis.

"I have lived and worked in the Lakes for many years, and in terms of perspective, it is important to remember the events of those few days were extraordinary. We knew there was going to be heavy rain and responded as best we could, but even our expectations were exceeded by what actually happened.

"I'm glad to say thanks to a lot of hard work all round and in partnership with various bodies and contacts, we are operating well again and very much looking forward to welcoming guests to the Lakes again this winter."

Currently around the county, a far-reaching £3.2 million action plan has been drawn up to deal with extensive damage to the county's vast network of public rights of way.

It means the Lake District National Park can repair or replace all of its 253 bridges and 85 paths destroyed.

In a joint initiative between the LDNP and Cumbria County Council, work is being rolled out in a four-year programme. It includes widespread repair and reconstruction, replacing gates, stiles and signs in a county boasting 7,500 km of footpaths, bridleways and byways.

The system - equivalent to Cumbria's total road network - saw £1.7m worth of damage caused in the national park and £1.5m throughout the rest of the county.

Dylan Jackman, from the LDNP, said: "An enormous amount of work has gone into surveying the damage and we are very grateful that external funding is now allowing us to get to grips with this difficult and costly operation.

"We are also determined to carry out the work in ways that will lessen the effects of future extreme weather. In particular, we will be looking at methods which will give us some flood resilience.

"Part of this process includes working with our key partners, including Natural England, the Environment Agency, National Trust, Forestry Commission and North West Development Agency."

Cumbria County Council, which played a key role in co-ordinating the exhaustive rescue and subsequent recovery process across the county, is planning to issue a 'year in review' update from Nov 15 highlighting what has been achieved and evaluated since the flood hit last year.

Around 2,000 locally sourced native tree species will also help protect vulnerable land around the Derwent and Greta rivers - which last November saw trees ripped up and carried away - and provide future flood protection.

The Environment Agency has teamed up with Bassenthwaite Lake Restoration Programme and the Woodland Trust to plant the sensitive sites with a range of indigenous varieties.

Project leader Mike Farrell, of the Environment Agency, said the Derwent, Greta, Glenderamack in, Cocker and Marron had already seen extensive action to stop loose soil entering watercourses.

He explained: "We have worked on a number of 'soft engineering' techniques, including planting willow spilling, fencing, hedges, even using large logs with small fir trees attached, creating a barrier to hold back eroded banks.

"These measures are very beneficial. Not only do they help improve water quality in Bassenthwaite Lake, but do well as flood defence by slowing river flows and helping prevent erosion. They also create new wildlife habitats.

"It was particularly reassuring to see how banks we have worked on stood up to last November's overwhelming floods."

A spokeswoman from Cumbria Tourism said:

"Last November's floods had a devastating effect on Cumbria's tourism industry, resulting in an estimated £15.4 million cost to the industry with over £2 million in lost and cancelled bookings.

"Research conducted with the tourism industry at the time and in the following months, confirmed that confidence about the year ahead was particularly low and almost 80 per cent of businesses believed that the weather had damaged trade with an average loss of 16% in annual turnover.

"Following on from the heavy rain in November, clean up attempts were severely hampered by freezing conditions and heavy snow through December and January.

"Tourism trade overall in the UK was down throughout this period but the picture in Cumbria was much worse than experienced elsewhere with occupancy levels down around 7% on the same period in 2008.

"However, the picture did start to pick up for serviced accommodation businesses in the Spring and occupancy figures from February to July were higher than the same period in 2008 and online bookings have been on the increase throughout the year. Cumbria Tourism's website www.golakes.co.uk has already had a record year taking over £2.7 million worth of bookings on behalf of the county's tourism industry, which also reflects the public shift of an increased internet usage."

"All in all, tourism businesses are resilient and have bounced back from the effect of the floods and despite it being a challenging year, visitor numbers have remained stable and we are cautiously optimistic going into 2011."

A Met Office spokesman said:

"Rainfall for the main event fell within a 36-hour period spanning two consecutive rain days from the evening of the 18th to the early morning of the 20th. During this period, the Environment Agency's rain-gauge at Seathwaite, Cumbria, provisionally recorded 316.4 mm in a 24-hour period and 377.8 mm in 34 hours. The current UK 24-hour (0900-0900) record is 279 mm recorded at Martinstown, Dorset on 18th

July 1955 so a comparison with this provides some indication of the extreme nature of this particular rainfall event.

"Twenty-four hour rainfall totals exceeding 200 mm are very unusual - there are fewer than 20 occurrences for the UK recorded in our database.

"Estimates by both the NCIC and the Centre for Ecology and Hydrology, Wallingford indicate that the 24, 48 and 72 hour rainfall totals have return periods of the order of 200 years, possibly higher. However, it is important to emphasise the significant uncertainty associated with return period estimates for extreme events."

ENDS

Weatherwise: The Lake District on record

•	November 2009: 314.4mm of rain fell in Seathwaite in 24 hours – a new record for England. Cockermouth and Keswick flooded.

•	7 and 8 January 2005: Storms batter Cumbria – a gust of 111 knots recorded on Great Dun Fell – many trees blown down.

•	Summer 1995: Drought year. Haweswater reservoir 89 per cent empty and the drowned village of Mardale visible.

•	31 Jan 1995: 100mm of rain overnight cause floods that change the course of Raise Beck - Dunmail Raise - to flow to Grasmere instead of Thirlmere Reservoir.

- July 1988: Grasmere had its wettest month of the 20th century.

- Summer 1984: Drought year. Drowned village of Mardale visible in Haweswater reservoir.

- Feb 1984: Over 600 mm of snow fell in some areas of the District.

- July 1983: Temperature in Ambleside reached 31.7C, the same figure as in 1934.

- 1963: Windermere completely freezes over.

20 TRIPLE CHEERS IN LONG PRESTON

ONE of North Yorkshire's oldest pubs with a history dating back to the late 1600s is preparing to celebrate its 315th anniversary in 2010.

Robert Palmer and wife Elspeth, originally hoteliers from Warwickshire, licensees of the bustling Maypole Inn at the heart of Long Preston, also recently celebrated their 25th anniversary at the pub/hotel, and the winning of the coveted Keighley and Craven District CAMRA Pub of the Season for 2009.

The stately inn, established by Ambrose Wigglesworth in 1695, is one of the most striking pubs on the A65, and still celebrates May Day maypole dances on the green in front of the square-fronted pub every spring.

Robert, a keen cyclist around the Dales, says:

"We're delighted to be looking forward to our forthcoming anniversary in 2010, on top of our recent CAMRA award, and on the back of our recent 25th anniversary.

"Long Preston has a proud history of welcoming both locals and visitors from along what was the old turnpike road for over 300 years, and we're the latest in the long line of that proud history.

"It's a lovely old building and especially in the spring and summer, and we're toasting to the next 25 years.

"It used to be known as the Eagle Hotel in the old days. A list of previous landlords and licensees going back to old Ambrose in 1695 is on show in the lounge and we're proud to be the latest on the long list.

"Some of them only managed to survive a few years and we've managed to outstrip most of them so it's cause for some celebration I suppose. Imagine what it would have been like in the 1700s with the horses passing through."

Robert was a publican in Canterbury before moving to Warwickshire and now Long Preston.

Occupation of the area around Long Preston, one of the most attractive of the villages which flank the snaking A65, dates back to prehistoric times. Remains have been found at Victoria Cave on the hills above Settle.

In 1086, Long Preston was known as Prestune, meaning "the priest's farmstead or town". Later on, "Long" was added, referring to its linear development and distinguishing Long Preston from the many other Prestons.

The first school built in the village was during the reign of Edward IV, around the time of the War of the Roses, which was part of the Hammerton Chapel.

In the War of the Roses, The Cliffords and the Percys, superior Lords of Craven, took an active part on the side of Lancaster during the whole contest. Many a man from Long Preston was lost as the Lords' retainers in Craven were obliged by their tenures to take to the field. After the bloodbath of Towton on Palm Sunday 1461, when Lord Clifford and 40,000 Lancastrians are said to have been slain, there would, no doubt, have been much mourning and lamentation in many a Long Preston household.

One villager writing in 1790 noted: "This part of Yorkshire…..was insulated from the rest of the kingdom, not so much by its high mountains as by its almost impassable roads. No wheeled carriages could ascent its rocky steeps, the carriers conveyed their goods in packs upon horses. The inhabitants of this hilly country were as uncivilised as their mountains were rude and uncultivated."

It was closed around the mid 1640s during the dissolution of the religious houses.

In 1695, at the time of the opening of The Maypole, William III, a Prostestant, of Orange, was monarch in England. A window tax was imposed in England, causing many shopkeepers to brick up their windows to avoid the tax. A war of a Grand Alliance was also being fought in Europe against the expansionary plans of Louis XIV.

Both the Maypole and the nearby Boar's Head, were both coaching inns serving travellers on the 'turnpike' road.

In the 1750s, the turnpike ran from Long Preston to Settle and in the 1960s this road, (now the A65) was raised, widened, and straighted. Several homes and farms were demolished to accomplish this.

Turnpike trusts were established in England from 1706 onwards, and were ultimately responsible for the maintenance and improvement of most main roads in England and Wales, until they were gradually abolished from the 1870s. There was a toll bar at Long Preston situated between Church Street and Bridge End.

The railway was first opened in 1849 and expanded in 1875 with the commissioning of the Settle-Carlisle Line. It declined in the 1970s and 80s but is now seeing an increase in heavy freight and passenger traffic.

In 1801, Long Preston's population was 573 and rose to 808 in 1831 but later dropped to 610 in 1961, most probably due to the end of the Industrial Revolution where people moved to the towns and cities to find work in the mills.

Between 1923 and 1935, the village was the railhead for the construction of Stocks Reservoir built by the Fylde Water Board (FWB).

Steam traction engines hauled material between the FWB depot, to the west of the current station, by road to Tosside where connection was made with a 3 foot gauge industrial railway system that served the dam construction project.

In the 20th century, most people were employed in the town at the garage, wool warehouse, auction mart, farms etc. or in the surrounding area, e.g. Skipton. A number of houses were rented at Long Preston making it affordable to live there.

In the late 50s and early 60s, there was a thriving livestock auction mart, shoe shop, tailors, butchers, bakers, post office, cafés, wool warehouse and corn mill.

A bypass was proposed and was given the go-ahead in 1994 after a great deal of money had been spent on planning. After the 1997 general election, however, with Labour gaining power, the bypass was plan was mothballed.

In the 1800s there were two pubs and two blacksmiths in the village; one situated at Anvil House, opposite the Boar's Head, and the other joined onto the Maypole between the houses on Maypole Green. The Boar's Head, on the Main Street, has hosts Darren & Paul Monks.

In the 1700's there were two inns; The Kings Head, (situated at the end of Church Street) and the Maypole. In the early 1800's the Kings Head closed and the Boars Head opened.

ENDS

- Long Preston's excellent own web site and a further history complied by R C Moorby can be found at http://www.longpreston.info/history/history.html.

- The Long Preston Wet Grassland Project, which began in 2004, aims to improve the wildlife value of the Ribble floodplain at Long Preston. The area floods every year, providing valuable habitat for wading birds and aquatic plants. The land is owned and managed by local farmers, who play a vital role in the project. The Long Preston floodplain can be easily seen from the Ribble Way, Settle-Carlisle railway and the A65.

21 A PASSPORT TO PERIL OR PROSPERITY

Almost five hundred years ago, the Yorkshire-born buccaneer and explorer Martin Frobisher risked everything in a bid to open up the elusive trade route the North-West passage.

Born in 1539, Frobisher, from Altofts, voyaged to the New World in what would eventually be a failed bid to open up the potentially lucrative Canadian sea route.

Now, it seems, not for the first time a Yorkshire man has been beaten in a quest to navigate an historic route.

For years, a trade route via the North East passage, the once ice-locked Russian cousin to the NW Passage, could only have been dreamt of by the hardiest of adventurers.

But now, thanks to a quirk of nature, climate change has unwittingly unlocked an elusive new route which some wonder could be the future rival to the Suez Canal.

Yorkshireman Jeremy Allison has been turned back by Russian officials in a failed bid to become one of the first sailors to navigate the stretch.

And on Sept 19, two German ships became the first Western commercial vessels to navigate the once treacherous stretch.

The passage is a shipping lane from the Atlantic Ocean to the Pacific Ocean along the Russian coast of the Far East and Siberia, sometimes called the Northern Sea Route.

The vast majority of the route lies in Arctic waters and traditionally parts were only free of ice for two months per year.

But climate change – ironically an environmental disaster - has meant the race is now on, in the best traditions of Marco Polo, to slash navigating times from Asia to Europe.

Traditionally, ships must otherwise navigate via the Suez Canal - a much longer journey.

It is expected the route will link Europe with booming Asian markets, slashing distances and journey times through the Suez and Panama Canals by as much as a third. Merchants could in theory then pass their savings onto clients, seeing lower prices in the high street.

In July, new NASA satellite measurements showed that sea ice in the Arctic was not just shrinking in area, but thinning dramatically.

In 1979 at the time of the Soviet invasion of Afghanistan, the route was largely impassable thanks to both the harsh extremes of nature, and the frosty patrols of the Soviets.

Russia has long used its northern coast for shipping fuel, supplies and other goods to its remote Arctic settlements, though funding for such shipments dwindled after the Soviet collapse.

Seventy-one-year-old Yorkshire sailor Jeffrey Allison, from Middleton Tyas in North Yorkshire, was attempting to become the first man to sail through the North East passage in the Arctic when he was arrested by Russian authorities while in their waters just days ago [Sept 20]

He was ordered to turn his boat around and sail to Murmansk, or risk being sunk by the coastguard.

He said: "It's bureaucracy gone mad over there . . . everybody was apologising for it."

Mr Allison and his two crew mates Barrie Beeken, from Melsonby, North Yorkshire, and Craig Longstaff, from Heighington, near Darlington, County Durham were attempting to negotiate passage and were 10 miles short of their goal when encroaching ice forced them to turn back.

On their return, around 30 miles from Norwegian waters, they were approached by Russian authorities in a gunboat, which told them they were in Russian waters.

The trio were forced to sail to Murmansk where they were arrested.

A Russian court found Mr Allison guilty of the offence and fined him 2000 roubles – about £40 – and had his visa revoked blocking the return to Russia for another five years.

Niels Stolberg, the president of Beluga, which is based in the German city of Bremen, called it the first time a Western shipping company successfully transited the North East Passage.

"To transit the North East Passage so well and professionally without incident on the premiere is the result of our extremely accurate preparation as well as the outstanding team work between our attentive captains, our reliable meteorologists and our engaged crew," Mr Stolberg said.

In Russia the idea of a possible seaway connecting the Atlantic and the Pacific was first put forward in 1525.

Warming has brought about the possibility of navigating the North-East passage without the assistance of icebreakers during the warmer part of the year.

Previously, Russian authorities would only permit vessels passage when assisted by Russian icebreakers, thus incurring prohibitive cost.

By late August 2008, climate change was such that for the first time in recorded history both the Northwest Passage and Northeast passage were open simultaneously.

Sir Martin Frobisher only found frustration and piles of 'fool's gold,', which he brought back by the tonne, in the environs of Frobisher Bay. His spoils, despite initial promising assaying, proved to be largely worthless.

Time will only tell if the new trade route across the wastes of N Russia will prove more lucrative.

22 WHATEVER HAPPENED TO THE SOUTH SEA BUBBLE?

The South Sea Company was a British joint stock company that traded in South America during the 18th century. Founded in 1711, the company was granted a monopoly to trade in Spain's South American colonies as part of a treaty during the War of Spanish Succession.

The primary element of trade was the Asiento, that is the buying and selling of enslaved human beings, in other words, the South Sea Company was essentially a slave trading corporation.

In return, the company assumed the national debt England had incurred during the war. Speculation in the company's stock led to a great economic bubble known as the South Sea Bubble in 1720, which caused financial ruin for many.

In spite of this it was restructured and continued to operate for more than a century after the Bubble. The headquarters were in Threadneedle Street.

The company, established in 1711 by (among others) the Lord Treasurer Robert Harley and a shady character named John Blunt, was granted exclusive trading rights in Spanish South America.

At that time, when continental America was being explored and settled, Europeans applied the term "South Seas" only to South America and surrounding waters, not to any other ocean. The trading rights were presupposed on the successful conclusion of the War of the Spanish Succession, which did not end until 1713, and the actual treaty-granted rights were not as comprehensive as Harley had originally hoped.

Harley needed to provide a mechanism for funding government debt incurred in the course of that war. However, he could not establish a bank, because the charter of the Bank of England made it the only joint stock bank.

He therefore established what, on its face, was a trading company, though its main activity was in fact the funding of government debt.

In return for its exclusive trading rights the government saw an opportunity for a profitable trade-off.

The government and the company convinced the holders of around £10 million of short-term government debt to exchange it with a new issue of stock in the company.

In exchange, the government granted the company a perpetual annuity from the government paying £576,534 annually on the company's books, or a perpetual loan of £10 million paying 6 per cent.

This guaranteed the new equity owners a steady stream of earnings to this new venture. The government thought it was in a win-win situation because it would fund the interest payment by placing a tariff on the goods brought from South America.

The Treaty of Utrecht of 1713 granted the company the right to send one trading ship per year, the Navío de Permiso (though this was in practice accompanied by two "tenders"), as well as the Asiento, the contract to supply the Spanish colonies with slaves

In 1717 the company took on a further £2 million of public debt. The rationale for the Government in all these transactions was to lower interest rates on its debt. It gave the South Sea Company (owners) a steady stream of earnings. The holder of Government debt got a new investment in exchange for terminating annuities.

In 1719 the company proposed a scheme by which it would buy more than half the national debt of Britain (£30,981,712), again with new shares, and a promise to the government that the debt would be converted to a lower interest rate, 5% until 1727 and 4% per year thereafter.

The purpose of this conversion was similar to the old one: it would allow a conversion of high-interest but difficult-to-trade debt into low-interest, readily marketable debt and shares of the South Sea Company. All parties could gain.

In summary, the total government debt in 1719 was £50 million:

£18.3m was held by three large corporations:

- £3.4m by the Bank of England

- £3.2m by the British East India Company

- £11.7m by the South Sea Company

- Privately held redeemable debt amounted to £16.5m

£15m consisted of irredeemable annuities, long fixed-term annuities of 72–87 years and short annuities of 22 years remaining maturity

The Bank of England proposed a similar competing offer, which did not prevail when the South Sea raised its bid to £7.5m (plus approximately £1.3m in bribes). The proposal was accepted in a slightly altered form in April 1720. The Chancellor of the Exchequer, John Aislabie, was a strong supporter of the scheme.

Crucial in this conversion was the proportion of holders of irredeemable annuities that could be tempted to convert their securities at a high price for the new shares. (Holders of redeemable debt had effectively no other choice but to subscribe.) The South Sea Company could set the conversion price but could obviously not diverge much from the market price.

The company then set to talking up its stock with "the most extravagant rumours" of the value of its potential trade in the New World which was followed by a wave of "speculating frenzy". The share price had risen from the time the scheme was proposed: from £128 in January 1720, to £175 in February, £330 in March and, following the scheme's acceptance, to £550 at the end of May.

What may have supported the company's high multiples (its P/E ratio) was a fund of credit (known to the market) of £70 million available for commercial expansion which had been made available through substantial support, apparently, by Parliament and the King.

Shares in the company were "sold" to politicians at the current market price; however, rather than paying for the shares, these lucky recipients simply held on to what shares they had been offered, with the option of selling them back to the company when and as they chose, receiving as "profit" the increase in market price. This method, while winning over the heads of government, the King's mistress, etc., also had the advantage of binding their interests to the interests of the Company: in order to secure their own profits, they had to help drive up the stock. Meanwhile, by publicizing the names of their elite stockholders, the Company managed to clothe itself in an aura of legitimacy, which attracted and kept other buyers.

A large number of other joint-stock companies were then floated on the stock market, making extravagant claims (sometimes fraudulent) about foreign or other ventures or bizarre schemes. These were nicknamed "Bubbles".

In June, 1720, an Act of Parliament was passed to control the Bubbles, requiring all new joint-stock companies to be incorporated by Act of Parliament or Royal Charter. This was commonly known as the "Bubble Act". It authorised incorporation of Royal Exchange Assurance and the London Assurance Corporation, so that the short title given to the act was the Royal Exchange and London Assurance Corporation Act 1719. The prohibition on unauthorised joint stock ventures was not repealed until 1825.

The passing of the Act added a boost to the South Sea Company, its shares leaping to £890 in early June. This peak encouraged people to start to sell; to counterbalance this the company's directors ordered their agents to buy, which succeeded in propping the price up at around £750.

The price of the stock went up over the course of a single year from about one hundred pounds a share to almost one thousand pounds per share. Its success caused a country-wide frenzy as all types of people—from peasants to lords—developed a feverish interest in investing; in South Seas primarily, but in stocks generally. Among the many companies to go public in 1720 is—famously—one that advertised itself as "a company for carrying out an undertaking of great advantage, but nobody to know what it is".

The price finally reached £1,000 in early August and the level of selling was such that the price started to fall, dropping back to one hundred pounds per share before the year was out, triggering bankruptcies amongst those who had bought on credit, and increasing selling, even short selling—selling borrowed shares in the hope of buying them back at a profit if the price falls.

Also, in August 1720 the first of the instalment payments of the first and second money subscriptions on new issues of South Sea stock were due. Earlier in the year John Blunt had come up with an idea to prop up the share price—the company would lend people money to buy its shares. As a result, a lot of shareholders could not pay for their shares other than by selling them.

Furthermore, the scramble for liquidity appeared internationally as "bubbles" were also ending in Amsterdam and Paris. The collapse coincided with the fall of the Mississippi Scheme of John Law in France. As a result, the price of South Sea shares began to decline.

By the end of September the stock had fallen to £150. The company failures now extended to banks and goldsmiths as they could not collect loans made on the stock, and thousands of individuals were ruined (including many members of the aristocracy as well the composer Handel). With investors outraged, Parliament was recalled in December and an investigation began. Reporting in 1721, it revealed widespread fraud amongst the company directors and corruption in the Cabinet. Among those implicated were John Aislabie (the Chancellor of the Exchequer), James Craggs the Elder (the Postmaster General), James Craggs the Younger (the Southern Secretary), and even Lord Stanhope and Lord Sunderland (the heads of the Ministry). Craggs the Elder and Craggs the Younger both died in disgrace; the remainder were impeached for their corruption. Aislabie was imprisoned.

The newly appointed First Lord of the Treasury Robert Walpole was forced to introduce a series of measures to restore public confidence. Under the guidance of Walpole, Parliament attempted to deal with the financial crisis. The estates of the directors of the company were confiscated and used to relieve the suffering of the victims, and the stock of the South Sea Company was divided between the Bank of England and East India Company. A resolution was proposed in parliament that bankers be tied up in sacks filled with snakes and tipped into the murky Thames.[3] The crisis had significantly damaged the credibility of King George I and of the Whig Party.

Joseph Spence wrote that Lord Radnor reported to him "When Sir Isaac Newton was asked about the continuance of the rising of South Sea stock… He answered 'that he could not calculate the madness of people'."

He is also quoted as stating, "I can calculate the movement of the stars, but not the madness of men".

Newton's niece Catherine Conduitt reported that he "lost twenty thousand pounds. Of this, however, he never much liked to hear…"

This was a fortune at the time (equivalent to about £3 million in present day terms, but it is not clear whether it was a monetary loss or an opportunity cost loss.

The South Seas Company's charter (of 1711) provided it with exclusive access to all of Middle and South America. However, the areas in question were Spanish colonies, and Great Britain was still at war with Spain. Even once a peace treaty had been signed, the South Sea Company was allowed to send only one ship per year to Spain's American colonies (not one ship per colony; exactly one ship), carrying a cargo of not more than 500 tons. Additionally, it had the right to transport slaves, although steep import duties made the slave trade entirely unprofitable. Nevertheless, relations between the two countries were not good, and the company's trade suffered in two wars between Great Britain and Spain.

The company did not undertake a trading voyage to South America until 1717 and made little actual profit. Furthermore, when ties between Spain and Britain deteriorated in 1718 the short-term prospects of the company were very poor. Nonetheless, the company continued to argue that its longer-term future would be extremely profitable.

The most commercially significant aspect of the company's monopoly trading rights to the Spanish empire was the 1713 Treaty of Utrecht's slave-trading 'Asiento', which granted the exclusive right to sell slaves in all of the American colonies.

Therefore, the primary trading business of the company was the forced transportation of people purchased from slave dealers in West Africa and sold into slavery in the Americas.

However, most commentary on the South Sea Company continues to focus on the money lost by English investors rather than the loss of family, friends, homeland, dignity, health and life suffered by the tens of thousands of people the company sold into slavery.

The Asiento set a quota of selling 4800 people into slavery per year.

Despite problems with speculation, the South Sea Company was relatively successful at slave trading and meeting its quota (it was unusual for other, similarly chartered companies to fulfil their quotas).

According to records compiled by David Eltis and others, during the course of 96 voyages in twenty-five years, the South Sea Company purchased 34,000 slaves of whom 30,000 survived the voyages across the Atlantic.

In other words, approximately 11% of humans transported as slaves died in transport. Employees, directors and investors persisted with the slave trade despite the on-going death toll, continuing through two wars with Spain and the calamitous 1720 commercial bubble. The company's trade in human slavery peaked during the 1725 trading year, five years after the bubble burst.

The Greenland Company had been established by Act of Parliament in 1693 with the aim of catching whales in the Arctic. The products of their "whale-fishery" were to be free of Customs and other duties. Partly due to maritime disruption caused by wars with France, the Greenland Company failed financially within a few years. In 1722 Henry Elking published a proposal, directed at the governors of the South Sea Company, that they should resume the "Greenland Trade" and send ships to catch whales in the Arctic. He made very detailed suggestions about how the ships should be crewed and equipped.

The British Parliament confirmed that a British Arctic "whale-fishery" would continue to benefit by freedom from Customs duties and in 1724 the South Sea Company decided to commence whaling. They had 12 whale-ships built on the River Thames and these went to the Greenland seas in 1725. Further ships were built in later years, but the venture was not successful. At this time there were hardly any experienced whale men remaining in Britain and the Company had to engage Dutch whale men for the key posts aboard their ships. Other costs were badly controlled and the catches remained disappointingly few, even though the Company were sending up to 25 ships to Davis Strait and the Greenland seas in some years. By 1732 the Company had accumulated a net loss of 177,782 pounds sterling from their 8 years of Arctic whaling.

The South Sea Company directors appealed to the British government for further support. Parliament had passed an Act in 1732 that extended the duty-free concessions for a further 9 years. In 1733 an Act was passed that also granted a government subsidy to British Arctic whalers, the first in a long series of such Acts that continued and modified the whaling subsidies throughout the eighteenth century. This, and the subsequent Acts, required the whalers to meet conditions regarding the crewing and equipping of the whale-ships that closely resembled the conditions suggested by Elking in 1722.

In spite of the extended duty-free concessions, and the prospect of real subsidies as well, the Court and Directors of the South Sea Company decided that they could not expect to make profits from Arctic whaling. They sent out no more whale-ships after the loss-making 1732 season.

Government debt after the Bubble

The company continued its trade (when not interrupted by war) until the end of the Seven Years' War (1756–1763). However, its main function was always managing government debt, rather than trading with the Spanish colonies.

The South Sea Company continued its management of the part of the National Debt until it was abolished in the 1850s.

23 A WALK IN THE WOODS

JUST at an age when most people are thinking they should be slowing down, one group of rural devotees has been picking up its picks and shovels to help keep the countryside spick and span.

Eighty-one-year-old Jack Jowett and retired colleagues, who form the Lower Wharfedale Working Group of the Ramblers' Association, are celebrating 15 years of putting their backs into repairing a broken-down collection of stiles, bridges, collapsed steps and gateways across Wharfedale and the Washburn Valley.

The group - which also counts members Walter Harford, Roger Stark, Jack Schofield, Barry Brand and the 'youngster' of the group Richard Smith (64) are all in their 60s and 70s and are retired professionals.

Formed under the leadership of Jack (Jowett), a sprightly 81, the troupe liaise with the major local authorities and landowners in the region to fill in the gaps in their rolling programmes of much needed repair works on the walkways of Wharfedale.

Since they were established in '94, the team has replaced or repaired over 260 stiles, 43 bridges, 75 paths, and installed or made good over 60 gates steps or fallen trees in the region.

Colleagues Richard, Barry and Jack (Schofield), pictured here installing a 'self-closing' walkers' gate on a much-loved footpath above Arthington, say much of the credit for the back-breaking work - should be given to leader Jack Jowett, a retired chartered surveyor, who has worked tirelessly - often in blizzard conditions - to improve the lot of the countryside.

Friend and fellow group member Barry Brand, paying tribute to him, says:

"Jack really has been the driving force of the group. He is well respected by all who come into contact with and above all he is a true gentleman.

"He took upon the task some years ago of identifying the problems on footpaths in the region which naturally occur with wear and tear over time; since then he has been approaching, on behalf of the group, landowners, farmers and councils to gain permission to work on their land and identify access points and necessary repairs.

"Materials have then to be sourced, which might include stile set planks or metal gates, and other tools, which have then to be transported to the site, often in his Jack's own car. And of course he has had to make sure everyone has been in the right place at the right time to start work. He's certainty dedicated."

Jack is modest about his own contribution but admits the workable liaison between the group and the councils and the landowners has been the key to success.

He says: "All the work is carried out by volunteers, occasionally helped by council footpath officers,

"We started because we felt the local authorities - certainly back then - were not perhaps doing the work on footpaths that we felt they could do, usually because of a lack of manpower and resources.

"When I joined the Ramblers' Lower Wharfedale committee, I felt the only way to get something done, practically, was to do it myself - and this is how the group formed.

"We get reports of the types of repairs needed from walkers and members of the public, and I approach the local authorities and landowners to organise a working group.

"The councils we are in touch with then provide the materials and we set to work. Today, we've been installing a self-closing gate, the benefits of which are obvious, but some of the largest jobs have been bridge repairs up to 5m across, say.

"We're obviously limited by what we can do in terms of sheer size, but the one thing we always do when we finish a job is to use it ourselves to check its safety and to make sure they are stock-proof with regards to animals."

"Eventually I shall give up - I'm 81 now, but there has to come a time when I pack away the tools for the last time. I just hope the Group doesn't collapse.

"Nine times out of ten it is the case that we respond to the parish council or a report from members of the public, but sometimes the local authorities will approach us direct. Farmers and landowners are often a source of info."

The group covers all the major parishes of the Wharfedale area.

Jack adds: "We're generally a good natured group but we can get a bit tetchy when the weather turns to driving rain - because it's horrible.

"We worked in whiteout conditions up near Little Almscliff one year - people were cross-country skiing past us while we were working away in blizzard conditions. But we got the job done as we had someone coming from North Yorkshire County Council who was a volunteer organiser so we wanted to show him what we could be done!

"The labour is always the thing that costs local authorities of course, and we can do the work far cheaper than if a council got the contractors in, especially on a bridge building, say. We carry out the work to their specification so it's a 'win win' situation."

The group normally meets throughout the year on Tuesdays.

Councillor John Procter, Leeds City Council executive board member for Leisure, says:

"The work of volunteer groups such as the Lower Wharfedale Group is greatly appreciated by the council and we value their contribution. By working together we can help improve and enhance the quality of the rights of way network for the future.

"We have developed a close working rapport with our volunteers and hope they enjoy themselves working together on a number of practical tasks, learning new skills and meeting new friends."

Leeds offers an extensive public rights of way network, together with other key strategic, recreational and permissive access routes, which together provide public access to both countryside and towns and villages.

The Lower Wharfedale Working Group of the Ramblers Association cover a large area of north west Leeds, where well known routes such as the Leeds Country Way, the Dales Way Link and Ebor Way cross the countryside of Leeds and also the council's Chevin Forest Park.

Public Rights of Way fall into differing categories and can offer access away from main roads principally to walkers, horse riders and cyclists.

Where possible, the council seeks to upgrade the surface and the structures that form the rights of way network so as to make the network more accessible to members of the public.

24 A GOLDFISH IN THE MURKY POOL

THE VICTORIANS are not necessarily the foremost group of people from history many would immediately regard as supporting a thriving enthusiasm for Islamic culture.

However new evidence unearthed by one of Britain leading English Literature academics suggests that some Victorian writers at least were not only tolerant of the religion, but regarded it with enthusiasm.

The findings, by Professor Francis O'Gorman, head of the School of English at the University of Leeds, look set to invert perhaps traditional held 'conservative' views of Victorian culture, literature and the period.

Professor O'Gorman, who recently edited a new version of Conan Doyle's famous Edwardian 'Hound of the Baskervilles' classic, suggests, with Islam being a frequent subject in media headlines for both good and bad, modern-day Britain could learn much from the Victorian attitudes highlighted in his research.

His findings are based on exhaustive research into the writers and period covering the late 1830s to the end of the 19th century.

Prof O'Gorman says:

"The Victorians, popularly famous as missioners, might seem unlikely admirers of religious faiths other than Christianity. Certainly, to many, they might seem unlikely admirers of Islam.

"The stereotype of the Christian missionary leaves little imaginative room, to be sure, to think of those men and women in the nineteenth century who thought seriously and sympathetically about the Muslim faith, and who found in its cultures inspiration for their own. But such men and women existed.

"The willingness of some Victorians to engage and think seriously about Islam I think is suggestive for today. It is, not least, a useful reminder to our own age.

"Thomas Carlyle, the great Victorian prophet of work and commitment, is perhaps the most important. He offered Mohammed as an ideal type of hero in his On Heroes and Hero-Worship (1841), one of the most influential books in the entire period. He was admired by Muslim scholars familiar with the West.

"Mohammed was, for Carlyle, sincere, passionate, and convinced that there was more to the world than material values.

"Others endeavoured to teach Victorian readers about Islamic faith. Even the Society for Promoting Christian Knowledge—an energetic leader in Victorian missionary work—published a careful, informed, and understanding account of Islam and Its Founder in 1878.

"The British traveller, poet, and critic of imperialism Walter Scawen Blunt was only one at the end of the century to write popular and accessible books in an effort to help Victorian readers better comprehend what it meant to be a Muslim and what political issues the Islamic world faced. His 'The Future of Islam' was issued in 1881.

"Creative writers and artists were not slow to engage with the imaginative potential of Islamic cultures either. An enthusiasm for 'Moorish' or 'Arabic' architecture swept England in the middle of the Victorian period: there is a fine example in St Paul's House in the centre of Leeds, built in 1878.

"Of the major poets to write on loosely Islamic themes, Robert Browning - whose archetypal 'Home Thoughts from Abroad' is perhaps the most celebrated ideal of Victorian works - is among the most significant.

"But for many his Persian volume, Ferishtah's Fancies, has often been forgotten. Ferishtah's Fancies is a set of stories about a dervish - a wandering Muslim teacher - which gently probes moral conundrums and asks readers to think open-mindedly about faiths most likely different from their own."

Professor O'Gorman says while the revelations are not new, the depth of his research suggests some Victorian attitudes might cause many today to lift an eyebrow.

"Thomas Carlyle is especially candid. He once wrote poignantly that the words Mohammed spoke have been 'the life-guidance now of a hundred and eighty millions of men these twelve hundred years. These hundred and eighty millions were made by God as well as we.' Christian or otherwise, that is an attitude which might usefully be remembered."

"I don't wish to take any political or religious stance on the issue, but as an academic, it's intriguing to see such open-mindedness in an era I'm sure many today would regard as being arguably insular by stereotype.

"I wonder how future academics and newspaper readers who study the latter part of the 21st century, its history and its writers, might view our current attitudes and epoch?

"We all look through 'a glass darkly' in history of course, but I'm pleased through these works and research to have glimpsed the odd goldfish in the murky pool of the past , and to gently highlight it.'

Coincidentally, the new findings come on the 140th anniversary of the birth of Yorkshire's R.A Nicholson, one of the founding fathers of the study of modern day Islamic poetry.

Nicholson, born in Keighley in 1868, was widely regarded as the greatest 'Rumi' scholar in the English language. Rumi was a 13th C mystic and Poet.

A lecturer in Persian, a Professor of Arabic at Cambridge University, Nicholson was able to study and translate major

Islamic Sufi texts into English. Sufism is said to represent the 'inner mysticism' of Islam.

His tour de force was his work on Rumi's Masnavi, published in eight volumes during the WW2 years.

He produced the first critical Persian edition of the Masnavi, the first full translation of it into English, and the first commentary on the entire work in English. This work has been highly influential in the field of Rumi studies worldwide.

His 'Literary of the Arabs (1907)' remains a standard work on the subject in English. He died in Chester in 1945.

Professor O'Gorman has been the Head of the School at Leeds since 2007 and specialises in Victorian literature. He is an advisory editor to the forthcoming Oxford Companion to English Literature.

The Victorian period was preceded by the Regency era and succeeded by the Edwardian period of Edward VII. The latter half of the Victorian era roughly coincided with the first portion of the 'Belle Epoque' of Western Europe and roughly the period of around 1300 AH in Islamic reckoning.

25 WAS LIFE SEEDED FROM SPACE?

SCIENTISTS are about to take the next step towards answering the controversial question of whether life was 'seeded' from space.

Astro-scientists have long harboured ideas that life might have evolved on earth, not through a natural organic process, but having been 'transplanted' from elsewhere in the universe.

As far-fetched as the theory sounds, space experts have long pondered whether comets and meteors are capable of carrying the building blocks of life.

Upon impact with the earth, or as the earth passes through the tail of a comet during its orbit, many have speculated that life - or at least the proto-chemistry of life – might have initially hitched an interstellar ride.

While the notion of 'transpermia' as the technique is known, has its doubters, a new probe is about to be launched to one of Mars's asteroids to test the theory.

A key stumbling block for proponents of the universal seeding theory has been whether tiny microbes could actually survive in the harsh environment of space.

At temperatures close to absolute zero, and being bombarded with interstellar radiation, many have thought even the most basic forms of life - if they did exist elsewhere – could not survive any trans-planetary taxi ride.

That's the question the US Planetary Society's Living Interplanetary Flight Experiment (LIFE) hopes to solve as it prepares to leave for the Red Planet in the next few days.

"It's a wonderful experiment," says Bill Nye, Planetary Society CEO. "This is the next logical step in answering the fundamental questions: "Where did we come from?" and "Are we alone?"

The Society is sending a collection of living organisms on a three-year trip to the Martian moon Phobos and back to Earth.

The Phobos LIFE biomodule is hitching a ride on the Russian Phobos Sample Return Mission.

Nye adds: "For example, if a rock on Earth contained life and were blasted off Earth, could it survive until it reached Mars? Or, if life existed on Mars, could it have been transported to Earth? The Planetary Society experiment will test the ability of life to survive the interplanetary voyage by flying organisms for several years through interplanetary space in a simulated meteor.

Inside the patented Phobos LIFE "biomodule," along with a larger soil sample container, are thirty tiny tubes, each just three millimeters across. They contain millions of non-pathogenic organisms from all three domains of life: bacteria, archaea, and eukaryota. The eukaryota include hundreds of plant seeds, and scores of tiny organisms called Tardigrades.

Seen under a microscope, hey are the most complex organisms making the round trip, which will last approximately three years.

David Warmflash is the Phobos LIFE Science Principal Investigator.

"We know that many of the species aboard Phobos LIFE are incredibly hardy," says Warmflash. "Many can be described as 'extremeophiles.'

"Some are quite complex, yet they can survive or even thrive in environments that are toxic for other complex organisms, such as humans. We can't wait to get them back in our labs to see how they've been affected by this especially challenging exposure."

Phobos LIFE will be the first test of organisms' long-term survivability outside the Earth's protective magnetosphere.

Almost all other such tests of space survival skills have lasted a few days or weeks. The handful of longer experiments were conducted in Earth orbit, well within our planet's strong magnetic field.

The magnetosphere deflects the majority of cosmic and solar radiation that makes interplanetary space so hazardous to complex life forms.

Scientists estimate that about one 'real' Mars meteoroid reaches Earth each month. More than thirty have been positively identified.

The biomodule itself is an impressive engineering achievement. Weighing just 88 grams, and easily held in the palm of the hand, it can withstand a 4000 g impact (4,000 times the force of gravity) without any leaks in even the first level of seals.

Phobos LIFE is mounted inside the sample return capsule, which will make its fiery descent to Earth without a parachute.

The spacecraft is carefully designed to land only on Phobos, and collect samples of the moon's surface, before the sample return capsule begins its long return voyage.

The Planetary Society's Bruce Betts is the Phobos LIFE Experiment Manager. "After years of preparation by our international team, it is exciting to be on the verge of launch," says Betts. "It's so gratifying to see the worldwide enthusiasm for this very low cost yet highly ambitious effort."

"In addition to the interesting science of the transpermia experiments, LIFE has a symbolic significance as the first directed sending of Earth life into interplanetary space."

26 BLUES FOR THE RED PLANET?

IN terms of voyages into the unknown, Mars is rapidly becoming the most jinxed planet in the Solar System.

The launch accident of the latest probe to Mars, the so-far ill-fated Phobos-Grunt probe, which has entered earth's orbit after veering off course at the start of its 33 day mission, will only heighten astro-scientists' anxieties about future trips to the Red Planet.

The probe, which suffered an engine failure at its launch from Baikonur in Russia, was due to land on Phobos, one of the satellites of Mars, and return soil samples from such.

Even for the most sceptical observers of jinxes, the statistics do seem to point to strange goings on with regard to voyages to the Red Planet.

In fact, the high failure rate of missions from Earth attempting to explore Mars has become informally known in the space and astro-watchers community as the "Mars Curse".

And the "Great Galactic Ghoul" is a fictional space monster jokingly said to consume Mars missions, a term coined in 1997 by a Time magazine journalist.

Of 38 launches from Earth in an attempt to reach the planet, only 19 have succeeded, a success rate of just 50%.

Twelve of the missions have included attempts to land on the surface, but only seven transmitted data after landing.

Britain's most famous Martian failure was Beagle 2 back in 2003-4 which lost contact after it separated from the Mars Express probe.

Prior to that, five of the seven probes sent to Mars have ended in failure.

The US's Mars Observer, Mars Climate Observer and Mars Polar Lander/Deep Space 2 missions all suffered either crash lands or a lack of contact, while a Japanese and a Russian probe also encountered problems either en route or on the hostile surface of Earth's neighbour.

The Mars Climate Observer's failure hit the headlines in 1999 when a a metric-imperial measurement mix up caused the probe to enter the atmosphere at too low an altitude, causing it to burn up.

The U.S,/NASA Mars exploration program has had a somewhat better record of success in Mars exploration, achieving success in 13 out of 20 missions launched (a 65%

success rate), and having succeeded in six out of seven (an 86% success rate) lander missions.

However in the late 60s and 70s it was a very different story.

The first successful fly-by of Mars was in 1967 by Mariner 4; but after that the US and the then Soviet Union failed in their bid to launch four successive orbiter probes to such.

Mariner 9 completed the first successful orbit in 1971, followed swiftly by the USSR's Mars 2 probe.

However while the latter successfully achieved orbit, its lander - which would have been the first to land on the Red Planet, also failed.

And while Mars 3 made a successful landing in Dec 1971, the first to do so, it ceased radio transmissions back to earth after just 15 seconds.

Mars 4 missed its orbit shot and only made a fly-by; Mars 5 entered orbit but failed to transmit data, and Mars 6 landed on Mars but again failed to transmit data.

And even the last of the Soviet ill-fated 'Mars' series had problems, its landing probe separating prematurely causing the probe to career into an irregular orbit.

It wasn't until July 1976 that the Viking 1 landed on the planet and successfully transmitted pictures of the Martian surface back to an expectant world in what could be described as being the most successful mission to Mars. Viking 2 also landed.

It perhaps goes without saying that the next scheduled mission to Mars - NASA's perhaps aptly title Curiosity probe - which is set to be launched on November 25 - will be scrutinised very closely on its voyage to the most unpredictable of planets.

The rover is set to explore Mars's suitability for possible habitation and will try to determine whether the planet ever did or could at some point support basic forms of life, among other planned projects.

○The majority of the failed missions have occurred in the early years of space exploration.

○Viking 1 and 2 were the most successful of Mars landers in the 1970s, while the Spirit and Opportunity Rovers have successfully scowered parts of Mars in recent years.

○The Chinese Mars Orbiter Yinghuo-1 was also sent with the current mission along with the LIFE flight experiment funded by the Planetary Society.

27 HAS LIGHT SPEED FINALLY BEEN SURPASSED?

In an ever changing universe, scientists have long used one great cosmic benchmark.

Since the days of Albert Einstein and his astounding scientific theories of the early 20th C, the speed of light has always been the great constant or 'speed limit' against which all others things have been measured.

Enshrined in his two great theories of relativity, scientists for years have long believed that nothing can travel faster than the speed of light.

The theory has been so long one of the great pillars of physics and cosmology that it has formed a fundamental cornerstone in scientific thinking, and underpins not only the great Standard Model of Physics but our basic understanding of the universe itself.

But this weekend at CERN, the home of the Large Hadron Collider, excited murmurings have begun about whether something which seemingly travels faster than light might have been finally detected.

And if it can be confirmed for certain, the scientific community might be forced to undertake the biggest rethink in its history.

In a specially gathered live webcast just this weekend, a team has been unveiling to an excited audience of scientists, and to the watching world, how the curious properties of particles called neutrinos might hold the key to the universe.

As a bi-product of on-going research into such, scientists working on the OPERA (Oscillation Project with Emulsion tRacking Apparatus) have been sending bursts of the tiny particles through the earth (using a neutrino beam supplied from CERN) to a laboratory at Gran Sasso, 730km away underneath a mountain in Italy.

To their immense surprise, preliminary results from the experiment suggest that the neutrinos – which like all things in the universe must obey the law of physics – may have arrived at the target site faster than a beam of light would have done.

Had the neutrinos observed Einstein's laws, the subterranean journey could not have taken longer than the 2.4milliseconds.

However they appear to have instead arrived at Gran Sasso 60 nanoseconds - 60 billionths of a second - earlier than light.

Not a great deal faster – but apparently faster nonetheless – which seemingly goes against science's most sacrosanct law.

The results are already sending ripples through the scientific community both at the site of the experiment at the cavernous halls of the INFN Gran Sasso National Laboratory, and at CERN, the source of the neutrino beams.

The results, delivered by Dario Autiero, from Institut de Physique Nucléaire de Lyon/CNRS were warmly welcomed by the audience watching this weekend's special lecture, though many are still sceptical.

'It is a tiny difference but conceptually it is incredibly important,' said Professor Antonio Ereditato, an OPERA spokesman.

"We have high confidence in our results. We have checked and rechecked for anything that could have distorted our measurements but we found nothing," Ereditato continued. "The finding is so startling that, for the moment, everybody should be very prudent."

The OPERA team were repotedly so cautious about their findings that they have conducted the experiment thousands of times over the last three years, and have opened up their research to other scientists working in the field. "We now want colleagues to check them independently," Ereditato said.

Yorkshire's Prof Dan Tovey, from the University of Sheffield, working at CERN, who is playing a key role in the ATLAS experiment as part of the Large Hadron Collider team, say the preliminary results are intriguing, but advises caution.

He says: "I would class this under 'extraordinary claims require extraordinary proof'.

"I applaud the initial suggestions but it is highly likely to be the result of an underestimated (or neglected) systematic effect.

"If we were to find particles which apparently travelled faster than the speed of light then this would have fundamental implications for the whole of physics - not least the fact that it would imply that in principle one could send messages backwards in time, violating the principle of causality (e.g. going back in time and killing your mother before you were born etc.).

"There are various weird and wonderful suggestions for how to evade such problems - but the fact remains that theoretically this would cause all sorts of problems. One then has to consider how this relates to other experimental tests of the maximum speed of travel of neutrinos, none of which have seen a similar effect of this magnitude.

"Particularly problematic is the fact that neutrinos from an stellar explosion not long ago called Supernova 1987a were observed to reach the earth three hours before the light from such…but this happened for well understood reasons.

"OPERA is claiming a 60 nanosecond advance over just 730 km by contrast. They state that their claim corresponds to an observation of a neutrino velocity greater than that of light by about 0.0025 %, while the SN1987 result suggests that any such difference in velocity must be less than 2 parts in a billion. So they're going to have to produce some pretty cast-iron evidence if they want to convince people that this effect is 'real'.

"Einstein's predictions and theories with relevance to light have been tested time and time again and while I don't decry the experiment, it would take something absolutely extraordinary for arguably the greatest scientist of our age to be proved wrong."

"This result comes as a complete surprise," said OPERA spokesperson, Antonio Ereditato of the University of Bern. "After many months of studies and cross checks we have not found any instrumental effect that could explain the result of the measurement. While OPERA researchers will continue their studies, we are also looking forward to independent measurements to fully assess the nature of this observation."

"When an experiment finds an apparently unbelievable result and can find no artefact of the measurement to account for it, it's normal procedure to invite broader scrutiny, and this is exactly what the OPERA collaboration is doing, it's good scientific practice," said CERN Research Director Sergio Bertolucci. "If this measurement is confirmed, it might change our view of physics, but we need to be sure that there are no other, more mundane, explanations. That will require independent measurements."

Prof Frank Close, professor of particle physics from the University of Oxford's Exeter College, and auithor of the bestselling book 'Neutrino' is also cautious.

He says: "Firstly, in my view, this isn't a discovery. It is an anomaly; they are actually just trying to find whereabouts some oversight might have occurred. In my opinion, it is important to recognise this subtlety.

"Secondly, they are having to measure both distance and time incredibly accurately, and any small error unaccounted for will affect the ratio of distance over time.

"I would reckon it is more likely that there is some yet-to-be included uncertainty in one or both of these measurements, rather than that their ratio rewriting the foundations of science.

"You can fire neutrinos through the earth but you can't fire a radio wave through and see which arrives first. So the measurement is indirect and there are ample opportunities for some unforeseen error to creep in. My bet is that that is what will transpire."

◦The INFN Gran Sasso National Laboratory (LNGS) is the largest underground laboratory in the world for experiments in particle physics, particle astrophysics and nuclear astrophysics. It is used as a worldwide facility by scientists, presently 750 in number, from 22 different countries, working at about 15 experiments in their different phases. It is located between the towns of L'Aquila and Teramo, about 120 km from Rome.
◦The underground facilities are located on a side of the ten kilometres long freeway tunnel crossing the Gran Sasso Mountain. They consist of three large experimental halls, each about 100 m long, 20 m wide and 18 m high and service tunnels, for a total volume of about 180,000 cubic metres.

∘The OPERA experiment is not actually at CERN - it's at the Gran Sasso underground lab near l'Aquila in Italy. CERN only provides the neutrino beam.

∘Albert Einstein's theory of special relativity holds that nothing can travel faster than the speed of light. The law was first proposed by Einstein in 1905, and its consequences are far-reaching - the c in the famous equation $E=mc^2$ is the speed of light in a vacuum.

28 A NEW TWIST ON ROYAL LINEAGE

While the recent announcement of the impending abandonment of male primogeniture might look to some to be the ultimate slap in the face to male pride, how different would England have been if it had been consigned to the historical scrapheap centuries ago?

It's perhaps futile to play the 'what if' game with history, but certainly, if the move eventually produces more female monarchs down the line, certain historians would not complain.

Royal watchers have long noted, in compiling the 'who's who's' of 'best' monarchs, that our queens - notably both Elizabeths, certainly Victoria, and perhaps less so Anne, would be close to the top of any monarchical hit parade.

The often-forgotten 'Queen Matilda' and Lady Jane Gray are also notable as the overlooked monarchs of England, among historians.

As for those near the foot of any prospective list, it's likely that King John (Lackland), Richard II, the largely ineffective Edward II and Henry VI, and to many Henry VIII - for many the very embodiment /victim of the male primogeniture statute - would be bringing up the rear.

But how different would England's history and royal saga have been if the males-first ruling had been abandoned in Henry VIII's time - and why and from where did it spring?

Author and historian Peter Algar, from Leeds, says:

"It might sound a controversial assertion, but it's not beyond the imagination to suggest that England could still be a Catholic country if male primogeniture had been abandoned in medieval times.

"Of course it is very much playing the 'what-if' game but it's not unreasonable to suppose that if Henry had been able to accept his first born daughter (Mary) as the 'accepted' future monarch, it could have saved a whole lot of trouble to put it mildly. Indeed he might not have had future children.

"The male primogeniture rule came to us via the Normans, this is where we get the expression taile male, (the Anglo-Saxons were more democratic in the way that they chose kings via the Witan).

"Ironically, the Hundred Year's War was started by Edward III of England after the death of his uncle, Charles IV of France. He laid a claim to the French throne on the basis of being his nearest male relative through the female association of his mother, Isabella of France, who was Charles's sister. The French crown had always been granted on male-line relations and there was, in fact, no precedent for claims through the maternal line.

Later, the Tudors "partial" claim to the throne was from the female line, the Beauforts (of the House of Lancaster). Their male line was not enough to secure them the throne. That is why Henry VII was keen to marry Elizabeth of York to cover all bets.

"His son, Henry VIII, was driven to have a male heir - as indeed many kings were in the period (and indeed) to this date; in fact, the familiar, if somewhat derogatory, phrase 'an heir and a spare' is still in use to this day in some Royal circles.

"Henry was famous for his drive to produce a son, to maintain his dynasty and of course he eventually did so in Edward VI, only for the boy to die at a young age.

If he had accepted - or was allowed - to accept Mary, his first born daughter, under an equality rule, it is fun to argue that he would not have divorced Catherine of Aragon.

"Even if you discount this, and accept his relationship with Anne Boleyn was triggered by lust, using the same train of thought, he might have been more accepting of their issue - i.e. Princess Elizabeth, the future Elizabeth I, and furthermore, might not fallen out with Rome over his desire or 'need' to marry Anne.

"Would England thus have remained a Catholic country as a result - and perhaps even to this day, if Henry has felt less 'constrained' by the statute of male primogeniture?

"It is perhaps a futile argument but if nothing else, it certainly serves to illustrate what could transpire as a result of the new moves. Seemingly innocuous changes in history have often had monumental effects, or at least the potential for such.

"In Henry's case, changes were afoot on the Continent in any case and Lutheranism/Protestantism would probably have held great sway eventually regardless, even if Henry chose not to establish himself as the supreme head of the church…but it's certainly a thought provoking argument.

"Mary of course did eventually become queen - but not until her brother Edward had been crowned under male primogeniture laws. When Mary did eventually take the throne, England briefly, though notoriously, returned to Catholicism.

"Henry's drive for a son - or indeed a child - is all the more poignant when you consider he married his late brother's wife (Catherine of Aragon) and traditional religious doctrine at the time suggested such marriages would remain childless. Henry never expected the throne, anticipating his elder brother Arthur would inherit such, and thus his drive for a male heir under the extant rules is all the more understandable perhaps? But how different it might have been in a more liberal climate with regards to future heirs.

History enthusiast and self-styled Republican Martin Gamble, from Bolsover, says

"The question over the effect of the proposed change is academic other than perhaps to give some traditionalists concern over the amendments to a raft of legislation that are required to several key pieces, including the 1701 Act of Settlement, the 1689 Bill of Rights and the 1772 Royal Marrriages Act.

"To bring the argument up to date, had the proposed changes been passed less than sixty years ago, Princess Anne would have remained as second in line to the throne before her younger siblings were born.

"Her son, Peter, would have been promoted to third in line at the time and Anne's daughter Zara, the eldest granddaughter of the Queen, would have been fourth in line to the throne.

"Since Anne and Anne's husband, Mark Phillips, refused to take Royal titles on behalf of their children, Peter and Zara, we could have had an interesting constitutional situation whereby an untitled person could have possibly become head of state!

"While not unique, a legitimate grandchild of a reigning monarch remaining untitled in terms of peerage is rare and has not happened for five centuries since the time of the Tudors.

"Peter Phillips married a Canadian Catholic, Autumn Kelly, who converted to the Anglican faith to ensure that her future husband would not lose his place in the line of succession.

"That act of selfless courage will no longer be required since the other proposals outlined recently will now permit a Catholic consort; although the interesting oxymoron of a Catholic head of state also being head of the Church of England remains an interesting possibility.

"Zara is now way back as thirteenth in line, behind her older brother and his daughter, the likewise untitled Savanna."

29 THE RIVALS

SUGGEST to the average Yorkshire man or woman that he or she owes a significant part of their proud heritage to the Lancastrians, and it would probably be enough to cause a riot.

While the story of the White Rose (and that of the Red) and the loggerhead rivalry between Lancashire and Yorkshire throughout the centuries is infamous in the north, historians have long known of a different story behind that of the popular saga.

Most school-children know of the bloody Wars of the Roses, and the clash between Lancashire and Yorkshire.

But historians who have researched the period are swift to point out that the actual clash – and ensuing rivalry – should more correctly be viewed as a north/south divide, rather than a geographical clash between neighbouring counties.

More surprisingly perhaps, it is being claimed that the so-called 'Yorkists' were actually largely Southerners, while it was the Lancastrians who held sway in the north – including the geographical county of Yorkshire.

Yorkshireman, author and historian Peter Algar, who has researched the period of the Wars of the Roses extensively, and who is an associate of the Towton Battlefield Society, says the truth is bound to surprise many.

He says:

"It's a popular misconception among many in Yorkshire that the Wars of the Roses were fought on purely geographical grounds – i.e. Lancashire in the west fighting Yorkshire in the east across the county borders. In fact nothing could be further from the truth.

"In reality, the conflict, at the time, was known as the 'war of the cousins' - not the Wars of the Roses - and it was between the HOUSE of York and the HOUSE of Lancaster which was more aligned on the north/south divide at the time of the bloodiest period of the wars, at Towton.

"The House of York at the time were largely southerners to a man; while it was the House of Lancaster which would have held sway across the North – and that includes using Yorkshire as a recruiting ground.

"It might be an unpalatable truth to some many die hard Yorkshiremen but our geographic county would most likely have been a recruiting ground for soldiery to serve the Lancastrian (ie. The HOUSE of Lancaster's) cause. Large parts of it were under the sway of the Duchy of Lancaster and the Lancastrian families of Percy and Clifford. Any "Yorkist" held land in Yorkshire at that time was extensively looted.

"The House of York members were the Duke of York (killed at Wakefield) and his sons Edmund of Rutland (killed at Wakefield), Edward IV, Clarence and Richard III (killed at Bosworth).

"The other leading Yorkists were the Nevilles of Westmorland and Warwick but they were prone to change sides.

"But the Yorkists i.e the House of Yorks's main recruiting ground for the common soldiery was the South (not Yorkshire) and parts of Wales and Ireland.

"It was only when Richard III restored favour in the north when he was governor here for quite a while during his brother's reign, and doled out wealth to his Northern supporters that the House of York had greater influence in the county. This all dissipated when Henry VII came to the throne.

"In my general experience as an occasionaly lecturer on the subject, the public – especially die hard Yorkshiremen - do not like being appraised of this. They have long held views of a geographic Yorks vs Lancs conflict. Look at the cricket and Leeds Utd v Manchester Utd or Leeds Rhinos v Wigan Warriors today.

"In reality, this was more of a North South divide and as uncomfortable as it may seem, we should celebrate our 'Northern-ness' with Lancashire.

"We held firm together during William I's harrying of the North, the WoTR, the Pigrimage of Grace and the later Civil War (as Royalists). As northerners, we don't like change, especially if it is imposed upon us from Southerners. But at the time of the Wars of the Roses, it was the 'Yorkists' who were the 'southerners'.

"As a possible modern parallel for today, we have a Duke of York - but he doesn't live in York and only occasionally visits there.

"Even more confusingly to some perhaps, the two houses didn't use the symbols of the white and red rose during the Wars of the Roses.

"During the battles, the Yorkist symbol was the 'sunne in splendour' - a triple sun or parhelion (which is a well-known astronomical effect sometimes called a sun-dog) reportedly witnessed by Edward IV, the Yorkist leader, before the battle of Mortimer's Cross.

"The Lancastrian symbol was a double S collar or a Swan – this is the imagery they would have used at the time – not a white and red rose.

"When Henry VII (Henry Tudor) ascended the throne at the end of the War of the Roses, his claim was tenuous at best. His link to the House of Lancaster, was through the Beauforts, an illegitimate relationship, that was later legalised to make the family respectable.

"He needed to secure his position beyond doubt, so he set his sight on Edward IV's daughter, Elizabeth of York to unite the two houses, bolster his claim to the throne and prevent further civil war. He needed a medieval marketing campaign to do this and his advisors came up with the idea of using the two roses as emblems, and then uniting them. This was how the red and white Tudor rose came to be.

"The symbols were given to counties during the Victorian period when they wanted to organise counties, boroughs and municipalities. In typical Victorian style, everything had to be grand. Sir Walter Scott was very popular at the time, and some say he is responsible for coining the phrase, the Wars of the Roses.

"There is a story about the Battle of Minden, on 1st August 1759 when a Yorkshire regiment, the King's Own Yorkshire Light Infantry, were fighting in Northern Germany and plucked white roses to commemorate their fallen comrades. That's why we commemorate Yorkshire Day on 1st August."

"The first record of a White Rose for the House of York (Roas Alba) was for the emblem used by Edmund of Langley, the first duke of York in the fourteenth century. The red rose emblem was used by Edmund Crouchback, the first Earl of Lancaster. This was the damask, Rose of Provins or Rosa Gallica as it was variably known, but as Edmund was born in 1245, this is way out of our period.

"All of this is not new to historians who have long known the real nature of the famous series of battles and the symbolry attached to such – but it's perhaps an uncomfortable truth for many a Yorkshire man and woman to know their ties with the those who bear the Red Rose are closer than they might have thought."

· Shakespeare has a key part to play in the use of Roses as symbols. In his history plays from the period, especially

Henry VI Pt I, Act 2 Sc 4, the warring rivals pluck white and red roses in the Temple Garden scene.

· Some editions of Shakespeare's canon list references 'The First Part of the Contention Betwixt the Two Famous Houses of York and Lancaster' rather than as Henry VI Pt I, II and III.

· Peter Algar is the author of the popular Yorkshire novel The Shepherd Lord, is an associate member of the Towton Battlefield Society and has lectured and written widely on the subject of the Wars of the Roses.

30 THE EMPEROR'S NEW CLOTHES: THE DIGITAL NEWSPAPER - THE FISH AND CHIP PAPER OF FOREVERMORE?

JOURNALISTS have a dubious reputation – there's no doubting it.

But a spectrum of such exist - those who are writer/journalists with more than half a brain cell writing for the quality press, the reflective outlets and associated blogs; those regional hacks and reporters who churn out the necessary regurgitations of the PR machine of the private and public sector and the 'still, sad music of humanity' as Wordsworth had it, and who occasionally reflect on such; and the rest who wallow in the mires of the tabloid press and its salacious happenings.

But don't deride any of them – as the Everyman of the press world, hacks from the quality press to the gutter press are actually just the mere reflective avatars of society. Occasionally the goldfish in the murky pool arises.

I started out in 1989 when newspapers were still king and the web was unheard of. My heroes were Clive James, Alan Whicker (!) and Alan Bennett and Melvyn Bragg, and the lesser known 'writers' of Gabriel Garcia Marquez and the acerbic and wondrously incisive Times food critic Jonathan Meades, who claimed to have put on an ounce for every restaurant he visited over fifteen years in the job.

Then something happened. People began switching on the web both at home and at work and a new revolution was born.

Newspaper journalists always used to refer to editorial as being news today, tomorrow's fish and chip paper.

Certainly my grandfather and father [demi-Hercules to me at ten going on 40] were so poor growing up in the Hunslet area of Leeds in the 1940s and 50s that they used to substitute what would have been today's cushioned velvet-like papier de toilette of choice with the slightly more robust torn-up squares of the Yorkshire Evening News on a hook in the outside toilet.

To those who know or knew them, they've come a long way since, but newspapers certainly made a big impression in the family in those days.

So much so that a visit to the doctor for a mal de derriere would often prompt a delay. When my grandfather asked if there was anything wrong as he bent forward, btm akimbo, the doctor would often reportedly reply: "No, I'm just reading yesterday's horoscope."

Newspapers were never destined to be items of latrinate liberation right from the start, - although it is open to debate - but have often ended up as the detritus of the everyday.

Many a time in the early 1990s I would merrily walk away with cod and chips wrapped in newsprint for two and unwrap a battered sausage for my wife to be, to which she would often remark with some delight that her portion was sheathed with one of my bylines.

I've not had fish and chips for a while – nor in fact mushy peas - but the last time I looked, the cod headline of the day wasn't wrapped around the haddock and extras.

Rather than being the fish and chip paper of tomorrow, thanks to the library like archive of the online, today's news has become more the piscatorial packaging of forevermore.

News which appears on the web, instead of disappearing down the same metaphoric gutter from which it came, now floats in the cyber space of eternity.

At last, a little like those movies which persist in the DVD hereafter – journalists are seeing their work float around the net – be it at times a cybersewer - for perpetuity.

Forever the yesterday's news men and women, today and tomorrow, journalists can at last glimpse what Wordsworth saw as Intimations of Immortality......or perhaps Intimations of Immorality?

In the days before she died, Marilyn Monroe, who herself knew the immortal nature of film, famously wrote a telegram declining a party invitation from Bobby and Ethel Kennedy, with the enigmatic lines: 'I am involved in a freedom ride protesting the loss of the minority rights belonging to the few remaining earthbound stars. All we demanded was our right to twinkle.'

Newspapers might not have the magnitude they once had, but perhaps at least, their writers and journalists and photographers - often all bravado nebulosity around a sensitive singularity - might just shine on.

♦ ♦

APOCHRYPHA – A NOTE ON QUANTUM PHYSICS

A short overview of quantum physics/a lay guide.

Until recently, quantum physics was a totally arcane and exotic form of physics only known within the high-brow circles of academia and to those who studied both the macro and micro worlds.

Even today, champions of such say the theory is almost unknowable, or so exotic that it can't be easy grasped or explained in just one sentence.

Background

In the old days of physics and astronomy, the old philosophers and observers such as Kepler, Ptolemy, Copernicus, and then Newton started to put their minds to how and why objects moved in the sky and what the forces might be which seemed to be controlling them.

In the Middle Ages of course, to the theologians and thanks to Catholic dogma, God - and 'man in His own image' - lay at the centre of universe, and everything circled around such.

They believed that there was an innate order of things in which the planets and the Moon (and moons) – moved around the earth on invisible fixed orbits, against a background of the stars – or the Primum Mobile as they used to call it.

Newton realised there was a force involved and called it gravity and developed his laws of motion to describe not only how the planets moved in the sky (and seemingly remained suspended there), but also how things moved on earth among a myriad of other theories. He's probably rightly described as being the father of modern science.

Einstein came up with two theories of relativity.

In the early 1900s– both the earlier Special and later General Theory – covered a wide range of subjects principally covering the constancy of the speed of light (in a vacuum); how everything is effectively relative to this; how to moving observers, (and that applies to all of us and every planet when you think about it) a given event can only appear to be relative; and the relationship between energy and mass; (they are interchangeable but crucially and 'magically' [my words] linked to the square of the speed of light).

His famous realisation of $e=mc^2$ led physicists to understand the high energies or potential involved in a tiny amount of mass – hence nuclear reactors and the atom bomb development.

(Einstein famously wrote to President Roosevelt warning him of the potential of his famous equation – which came prophetically true).

But perhaps his greatest concept, in his second General Theory, was that of space-time. In this he took Newton's studies of gravity and successfully amended them to incorporate them with his earlier Special Theory of Relativity.

Aside from the three dimensions of space we know, he added a 'fourth' dimension, called space-time in which gravity, light, time and the three physical properties of space were seemingly inter linked.

Until the beginning of the 20th century, time was believed to be independent of motion, progressing at a fixed rate in all reference frames; however, later experiments revealed that time slowed down at higher speeds of the reference frame relative to another reference frame (with such slowing called "time dilation" explained in the theory of "special relativity").

Many experiments have confirmed time dilation, such as atomic clocks on board a Space Shuttle running slower than synchronized Earth-bound inertial clocks.

The duration of time can therefore vary for various events and various reference frames.

The classic example of this is the so called twin paradox.

If you happen to have a moped that can travel at the speed of light, and you are sat with your friend in the city plaza having a coffee, imagine you run out of sugar.

Your pal, who happens to know that the best sugar in the universe [say] lies on Proxima Centauri, says: "Hang on, I'll just nip and get some".

Now Proxima Centauri is four light years away. So say your pal speeds on his hyper cycle, travelling at the speed of light. It takes him four years to get there and four years to get back.

Measuring the time he is gone on HIS watch, he has been gone eight years.

But on his return to the city plaza, not only has his waiting coffee gone cold, but you have turned to dust and perhaps a 100 years have passed in 'earth time', even though your pal seemed only to be gone for eight years.

These are just some of the strange effects of time dilation when objects approach the speed of light which Einstein predicted.

Einstein also predicted that heavy objects in space should actually 'warp' the fabric of space through their sheer mass and gravitational effect. And not only that, but a distortion of time would be involved for observers of such.

As far-fetched as this may seem, he was proved to be correct in a famous experiment conducted later when astronomers and physicists observed the sun during an eclipse.

Einstein predicted that the best way to test the idea of the warping of space-time by heavy objects would be if we could observe the light coming from a star which lies beyond some huge beyond huge mass was warping the fabric of space-time.

A bit like the effect of dipping a spoon in water (which appears bent from certain angles), the light from the star beyond the mass (the sun say), he said, should be bent or distorted by the huge space-time gravity well in which the sun sits - and thus the star should actually appear to be in a different position.

In the above, the light rays from the distant star are bent around the space-time gravity well created by the mass of the Sun, to such an extent that to the observer, the star beyond the sun, tracing back along the line of the light, appears to be in a different position.

Of course, you can't see light from stars beyond the sun because the sun is too bright – it masks most stars.

But in a famous experiment by Arthur Eddington, the results were confirmed during a solar eclipse confirming the bending of light around massive objects.

The result in about 1919 'proved' this aspect of relativity and made headline news across the world.

Newton had originally come up with the theory, but Einstein's predictions were so accurate – confirmed later by Eddington – that relativity - rather than replacing Newton's theory's – simply built on top of them.

Enter the quantum world.

So everything seemed quite predictable on the classical large scale – Newton and Einstein's theories - building on top of other theories - , seemed to give science the upper hand.

For the first time in the history of mankind in the early 1900s, science seemed to have in place a series of theories which not only approached an approximation of how the observable universe worked (or certainly the motion of things within it), but which enabled a set of theories and laws which actually seemed remarkably accurate.

Scientists in a sense for the first time, could perhaps legitimately describe themselves as having divined the mind of God [whether or not he existed].

Through sheer reasoning, mathematics and observation – a so-called pragmatic approach – man could seemingly fathom the vastness of space.

But then in the 1920 something happened which would literally throw the cat among the pigeons.

The discovery of atomic structure and the protons, neutrons and electrons which underlie the principle elements of nature caused scientists to probe deeper into the heart of things.

Atomic structure revealed that the basic elements were made of protons, neutrons and electrons.

The protons and neutrons (collectively known as hadrons) have within them quarks, which to date seem to be the fundamental constituents of matter.

Quantum mechanics is based upon the concept that subatomic particles can have both wave-like and particle-like properties.

This phenomenon is known as wave–particle duality.

The explanation stems from a theory proposed by French physicist Louis de Broglie in 1924, that subatomic particles such as electrons are associated with waves.

The concept of waves and particles, and the analogies which use them, are mechanisms of classical physics.

Unfortunately, quantum mechanics, which seeks to explain nature at a level underlying that of the atoms which comprise matter, cannot be understood in such terms.

Suppose that we want to measure the position and speed of an object -- for example a car going through a radar speed trap.

Naively, we assume that (at a particular moment in time) the car has a definite position and speed, and how accurately we can measure these values depends on the quality of our measuring equipment.

If we improve the precision of our measuring equipment, we will get a result that is closer to the true value.

In particular, we would assume that how precisely we measure the speed of the car does not affect its position, and vice versa.

In 1927 German physicist Werner Heisenberg proved that in the sub-atomic world such assumptions are not correct.

Quantum mechanics shows that certain pairs of physical properties, such as position and speed, cannot both be known to arbitrary precision i.e. at the same time.

He showed that the more precisely one of them is known, the less precisely the other can be known.

This statement is known as the Uncertainty Principle (or Heisenberg's uncertainty principle).

It is not a statement about the accuracy of our measuring equipment, but about the nature of the system itself – i.e. our naive assumption that an object has a definite position and speed, is incorrect.

Scientists now realise that on a scale of cars and people and planets, i.e. the classical level, these uncertainties are still present but are too small to be noticed; yet these uncertainties are large enough that when dealing with individual atoms and electrons they become critical.

Simply put, on the large scale, the classical laws of Einstein and Newton seem to hold.

But at the heart of things, on the very subatomic level, not only do these laws seem to break down or be wildly inaccurate, but chance and chaos seems to reign.

In other words, there seems to be a fundamental uncertainty at the heart of things, and it was this concept which Heisenberg encapsulated in his Uncertainty Principle.

Einstein disliked the ideas of quantum theory claiming that 'God does not play dice'; and yet he later acknowledged – and sought to bring together - his theories of relativity with quantum mechanics.

Just as Newton was never satisfied with his theory of gravity, Einstein was never satisfied with General Relativity (his second theory).

Einstein was disturbed by two problems: he believed that there should be just one theory to account for both gravity and electro-magnetism, and he believed that this "unified field" theory should get rid of quantum mechanics.

Although Einstein himself helped create quantum mechanics, he hated the very notion until his death.

One interpretation of quantum mechanics is that everything is uncertain, and everything is fundamentally governed by the laws of probability.

Much has happened since Einstein's day – principally the realisations of the four fundamental forces in the universe (or the four fundamental forces of 'Nature').

These are: gravity; the strong nuclear force (the binding energy or glue which holds protons and neutrons together); the weak nuclear force (which is crucial to radioactive decay), and electromagnetism.

Many people [and certainly older high school children] are probably familiar with the link between magnetism and electricity.

An understanding of the relationship between electricity and magnetism began in 1819 with work by Hans Christian Oersted, a professor at the University of Copenhagen, who discovered more or less by accident that an electric current could influence a compass needle.

Several other experiments followed, with André-Marie Ampère, who in 1820 discovered that the magnetic field circulating in a closed-path was related to the current flowing through the perimeter of the path.

Michael Faraday, in 1831 found that magnet passed through a loop of wire, induced a voltage; James Clerk Maxwell synthesized and expanded these insights into Maxwell's equations, unifying electricity, magnetism, and optics into the field of electromagnetism. In 1905, Einstein used these laws in motivating his theory of special relativity, requiring that the laws held true in all inertial reference frames.

The weak nuclear force, the second of the four fundamental forces, is responsible for the radioactive decay of subatomic particles and initiates the process known as hydrogen fusion in stars – the massive nuclear conversion process which lies at the heart of glowing stars, which essential convert hydrogen into helium.

In 1968, the electromagnetic force and the weak nuclear force or interaction were 'unified', when they were shown to be two aspects of a single force, now termed the electro-weak force.

Many theorists today are trying to unify fully the four fundamental forces in the universe – and the Large Hadron Collider (which literally smashes protons together at high energies) is proving crucial in unveiling both new particles and new realms in which the fundamental forces of everything start to come together.

Physicists refer a 'Standard Model of Physics' which incorporates all the major force particles and sub atomic particles which seem to fit together well. The missing jigsaw piece currently is the Higgs Boson which they hope the LHC will unveil and which is crucial to understanding 'mass'.

However, the full realisation of many is that the final unification of the four forces – known as the Theory of Everything – can only truly have happened at the moment of the Big Bang when the energies involved were absolutely colossal. In fact language probably has no means to encapsulate what actually happened there.

The Theory of Everything

Just as years ago scientists realised a link between electricity and magnetism to form electro-magnetism, today they are trying to unify the four fundamental forces in the universe.

On the ultimate level, a 'Theory of Everything' would unify all the fundamental interactions of nature: gravitation, strong nuclear force, weak nuclear force, and electromagnetism

Several (lesser!) so called Grand Unified Theories (GUTs) have been proposed to unify three of these forces - electromagnetism and the weak and strong forces. Remember two of these themselves have already been unified (electromagnetism and the weak nuclear force) – the so called electro weak theory.

Although these two forces appear very different at everyday low energies, the theory models them as two different aspects of the same force.

Above the unification energy, on the order of 100 GeV, they would merge into a single electroweak force.

Thus if the universe is hot enough (approximately 1015 K, a temperature exceeded until shortly after the Big Bang) then the electromagnetic force and weak force will merge into a combined electroweak force.

Grand unification would imply the existence of an electronuclear force; it is expected to set in at energies of the order of 1016 GeV, far greater than could be reached by any possible Earth-based particle accelerator.

Yet GUTs are clearly not the final answer; both the current standard model and all proposed GUTs are quantum field theories. i.e. the final step in the graph requires resolving the separation between quantum mechanics and gravitation, often equated with general relativity.

Numerous researchers concentrate their efforts on this specific step; nevertheless, no accepted theory of 'quantum gravity' – and thus no accepted theory of everything – has emerged yet.

In addition to explaining the forces listed in the graph, a TOE must also explain the status of at least two candidate forces suggested by modern cosmology: an inflationary force and dark energy.

Furthermore, cosmological experiments also suggest the existence of dark matter, supposedly composed of fundamental particles outside the scheme of the standard model. However, the existence of these forces and particles has not been proven yet.

Note on Schrodinger's Cat.

One of the oddest bi-products of quantum discussions – and the realisation that on the small scale particles can appear to be in a quantum or seemingly random state or position (called superposition) is the arcane thought experiment known as Schrodinger's Cat.

The thought experiment serves to illustrate the bizarreness of quantum mechanics and the mathematics necessary to describe quantum states.

Schrödinger's Cat: A cat, along with a flask containing a poison and a radioactive source, is placed in a sealed black box.

At one side inside the box is a tiny atomic source which over the course of an hour may or may not decay.

If an internal Geiger counter detects radiation, the flask is automatically shattered by a hammer mechanism releasing the poison that kills the cat.

If it doesn't decay in the hour, the flask remains intact and the cat remains alive.

Schrodinger argued that over the course of one hour, in essence, an external observer one could not for certain predict whether the cat was 'alive or dead' (without opening the box). He argued to all intents and purposes it was in a 'quantum state' i.e. alive/dead.

Only by opening the box do we actually ascertain for certain whether the cat is alive OR dead – but the downside of all this is that we have broken the 'quantumness' of the system.

However esoteric this might seem, many volumes have been written on this hypothesis. It has also been used to question where the reality boundary lies between the 'quantum world' and the 'classical' macro boundary of the likes of Einstein and Newton.

Nobel prizes lie in wait for those who can discover such.

MH 2011

ACKNOWLEDGEMENTS

For help and encouragement with the attached, I'm very grateful to those at the Yorkshire Post, the Guardian, Country Publications, the Catholic Times, the BBC and a host of other media outlets in the north. Special thanks must be given to Prof Frank Close, Prof Francis O'Gorman, Paul Jackson, Sarah Freeman, Peter Charlton, Peter Algar, Chris Rae, Seth Shostak, Prof Lisa Hopkins, Ian McMillan, journalist John Baron; and especially to my father David Hickes, and my long suffering wife Helen, and daughter Meg, and my lovely mum Christine…without whom…

Special thanks are also due to Tim Stubbs, John Bareham, and the late Piers Hampton, and Tim Hughes and all from the old 'Diogenes' club; David Hill, and all of the old Hickes 'mafia' for their support both past and present.

© Martin Hickes 2011

ABOUT THE AUTHOR

Martin Hickes trained as a journalist in 1989 after gaining a 2:1 in English Literature at university in Sheffield. Since then he has written widely for both print and online for the media in the N of England, and undertaken a significant degree of PR work. He was taught by the poet Ian McMillan among others and grew up in Pool in Wharfedale, near Leeds, an inspiration for many of his works and writings. He is a devout fan of the works of Monty Python, Douglas Adams, William Shakespeare, Clive James, Bill Bryson and all things entomological. He enjoys the humour of *Blackadder, Yes Minister/Yes, Prime Minister,The Phil Silvers Show (Sgt Bilko) and Laurel and Hardy.* As a kid, he grew up watching the ground-breaking series *Cosmos*, with Carl Sagan, sparking a long-standing, if lay, interest in science, space, particle physics, and the 'big picture'.

© Martin Hickes/Tudor Close Publications
All rights reserved.

Logo design courtesy © Martin Williamson (with permission).

Cover photography David Hickes – Ladymere from Lake Windermere

A Goldfish in the Murky Pool

Martin Hickes

A Goldfish in the Murky Pool

Proof

Made in the USA
Charleston, SC
05 December 2011